# Drawing from a Parallel Universe

*Realistic Templates for the Beginning Artist*

Text and Illustrations by
Peggy Strickland

The prints available in this volume were created using original
photographs by the author, digitally rendered to display in "coloring
book form."

# Table of Contents

*True artistry arises from within, subjective to the perhaps slanted perception, bias, skill and vision unique to the artist.*

Consider that you, as a fledgling artist, believe that some creative genius resides within you. How do you focus that creativity to allow expression as quality artwork? How do you broach the vast whiteness of a daunting, blank canvas?

Quite simply; how do you begin?

Some of the most realistic paintings are derived from photographs; either those the artist develops for ease of subject matter (like living creatures, in constant motion) or from pictures that just happen to appeal to the artistic eye, begging to be painted.

The following renditions offer photographic precision combined with the very basic in template design.

With your own brush strokes or pencil transfer the gray and white images to your sketchpad or canvas, or simply color in or paint on the printed template.

*For ease of use, and to grant your own visionary impression full freedom of expression, a very minimal use of instructional text accompanies these prints.

So, get out those sketch pads, pencils, brushes and paints and, taking a few simple cues from Nature, allow your creative whimsy free reign and true artistic expression!

***Plants and flowers*** present unique opportunities for expression of personal perception.

Individual techniques for brush strokes and delicate color shadings can produce widely varying impressionistic drawings and paintings.

~~~~~~~

Do not hamper creativity by imposing ***unrealistic*** expectations for realistic appearance in your interpretation of nature's infinite beauty.

~~~~~~~

The photographic nature of the templates found herein offer possibilities limited not by your palette, but by those boundaries you set on your own imagination.

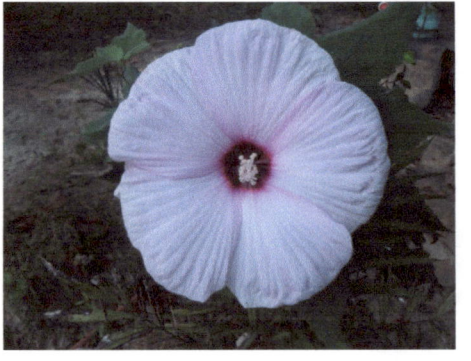 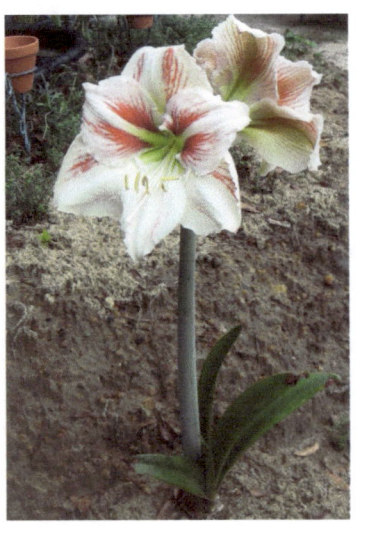

From the slightly frilled edges of a stately Amaryllis

to the deep, velvet throat of the exquisite Hibiscus,

hues and textures
ripple
and
flow.

***

**Amaryllis**

**In**

**Full**

**Blooming**

**Glory**

***

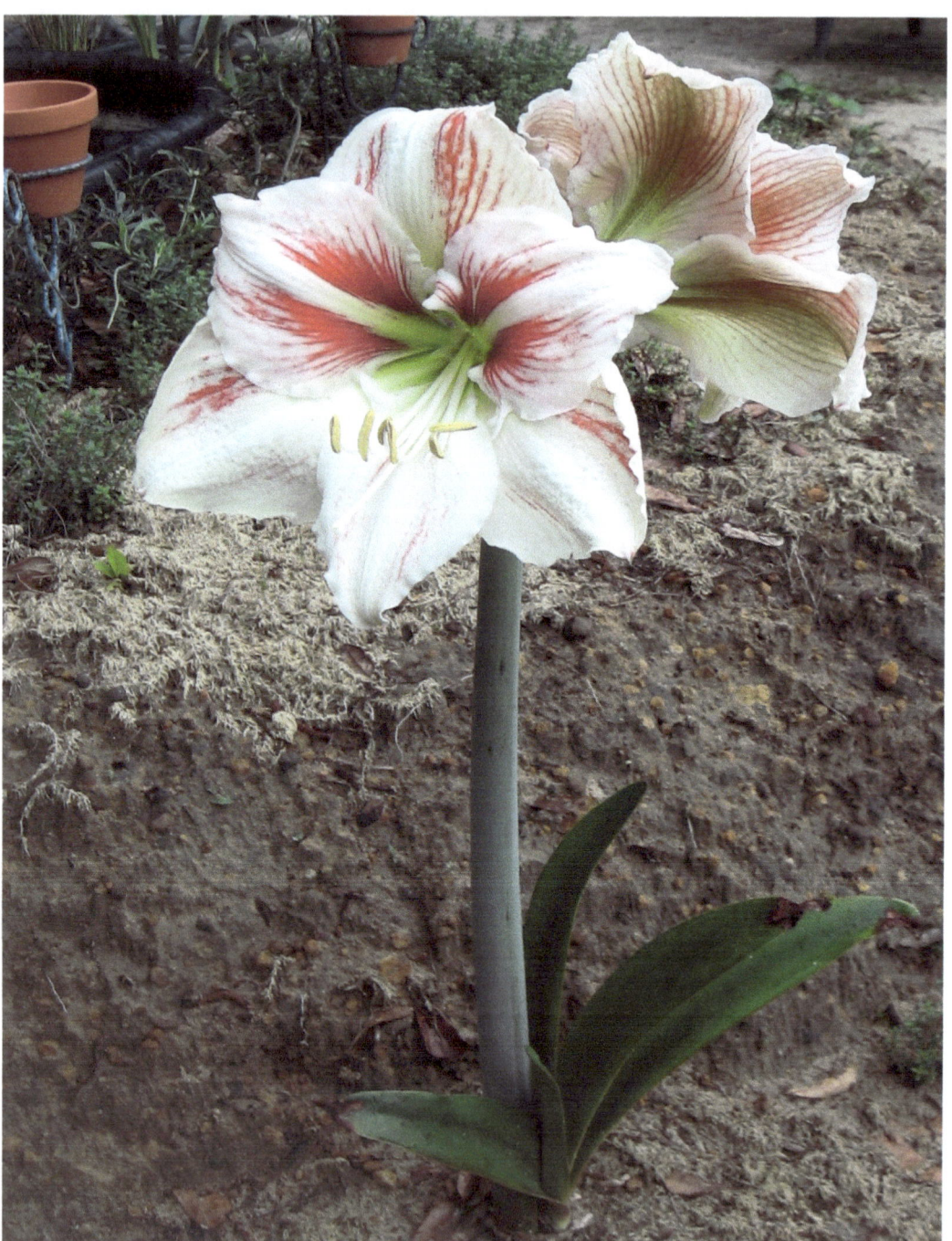

When sketching the outlines
for your plants, flowers or
trees, use a feathery touch
with your pencil or brush.

Petals or leaves should be
darker near the center,
blending to edges that are
sometimes hinted at,
rather than expressed
by definitive lines.

Some lines have been
Added to this template as
a visual aid.

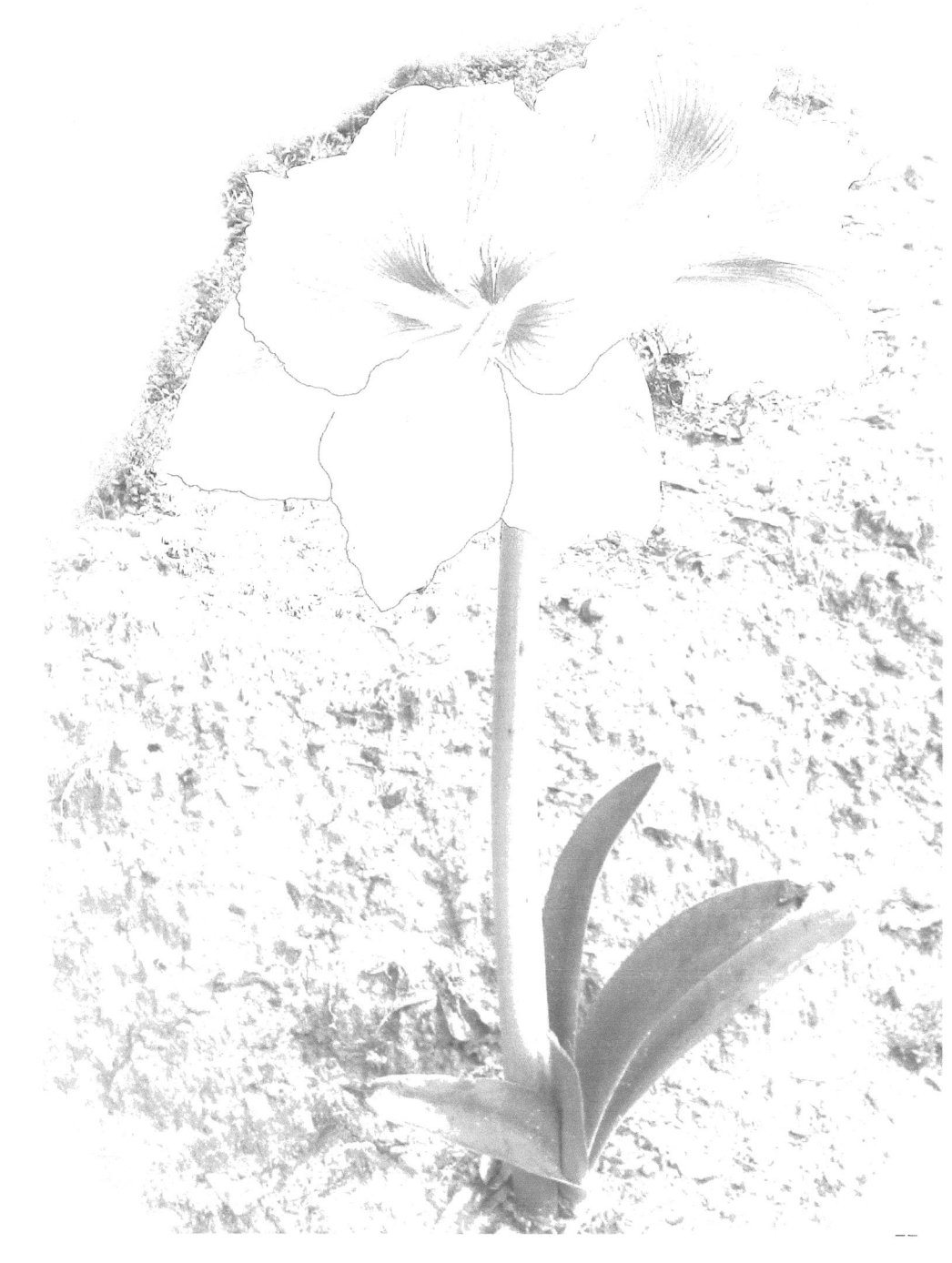

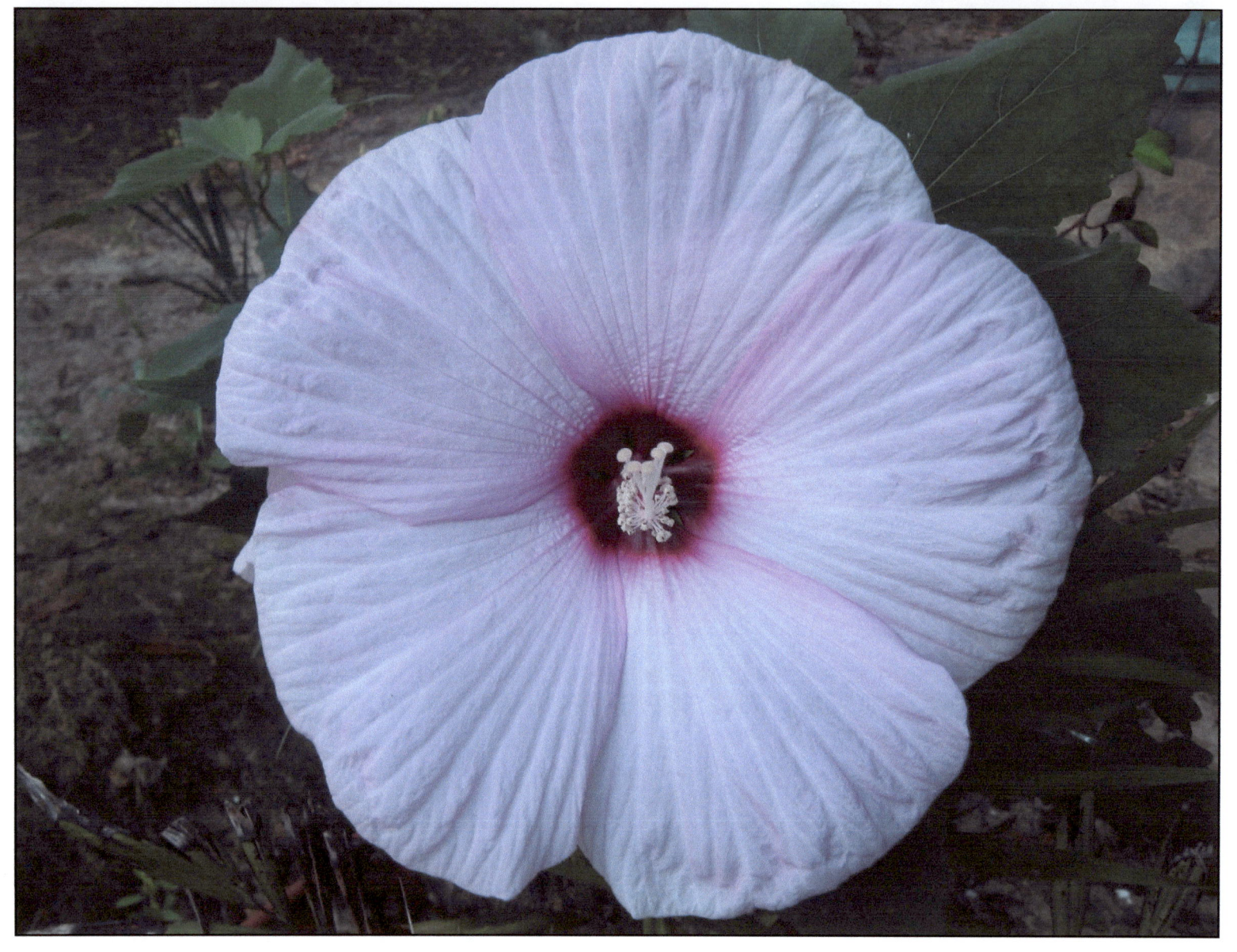

Magnificent Dinner Plate Hibiscus

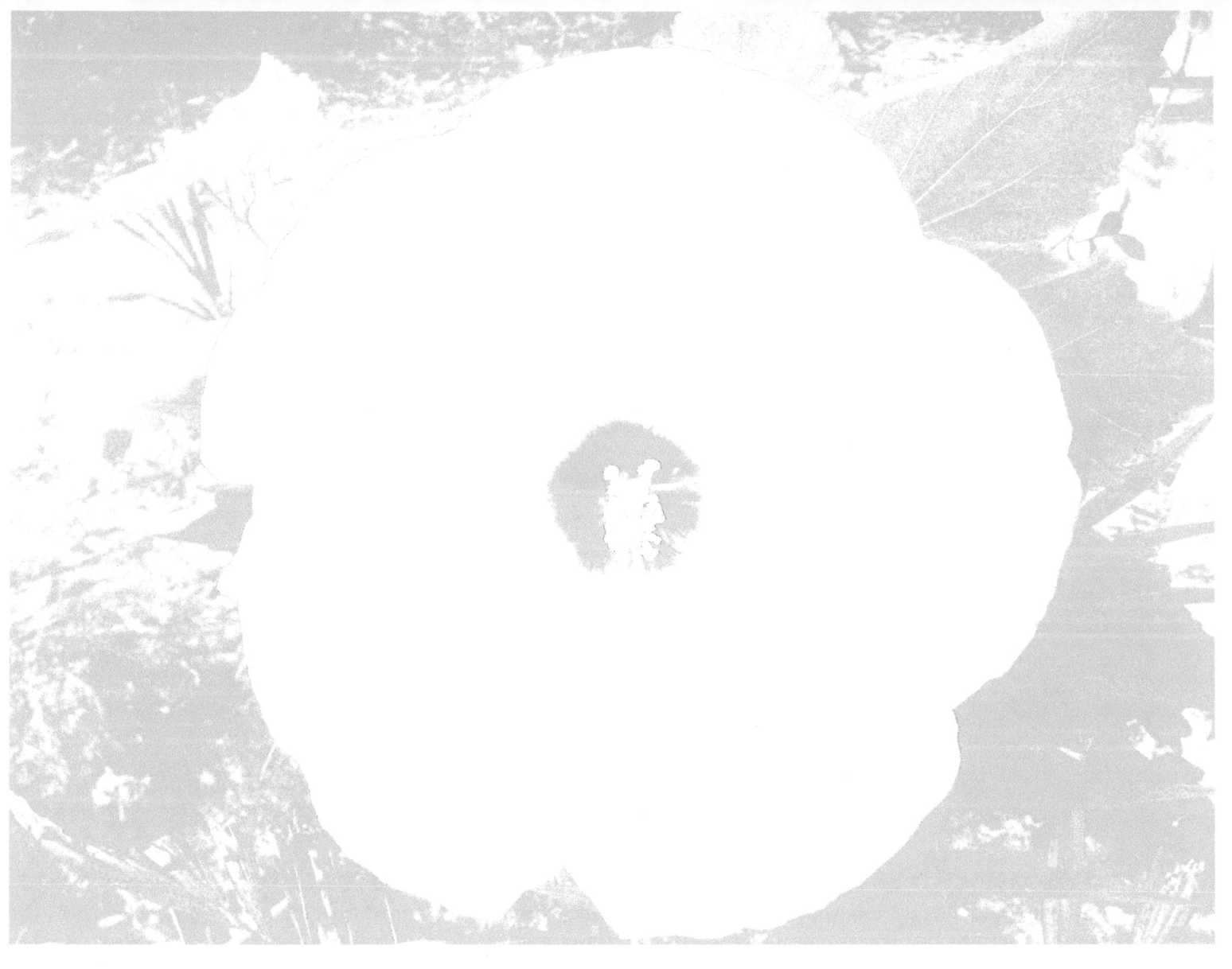

A bare outline image invites creativity.

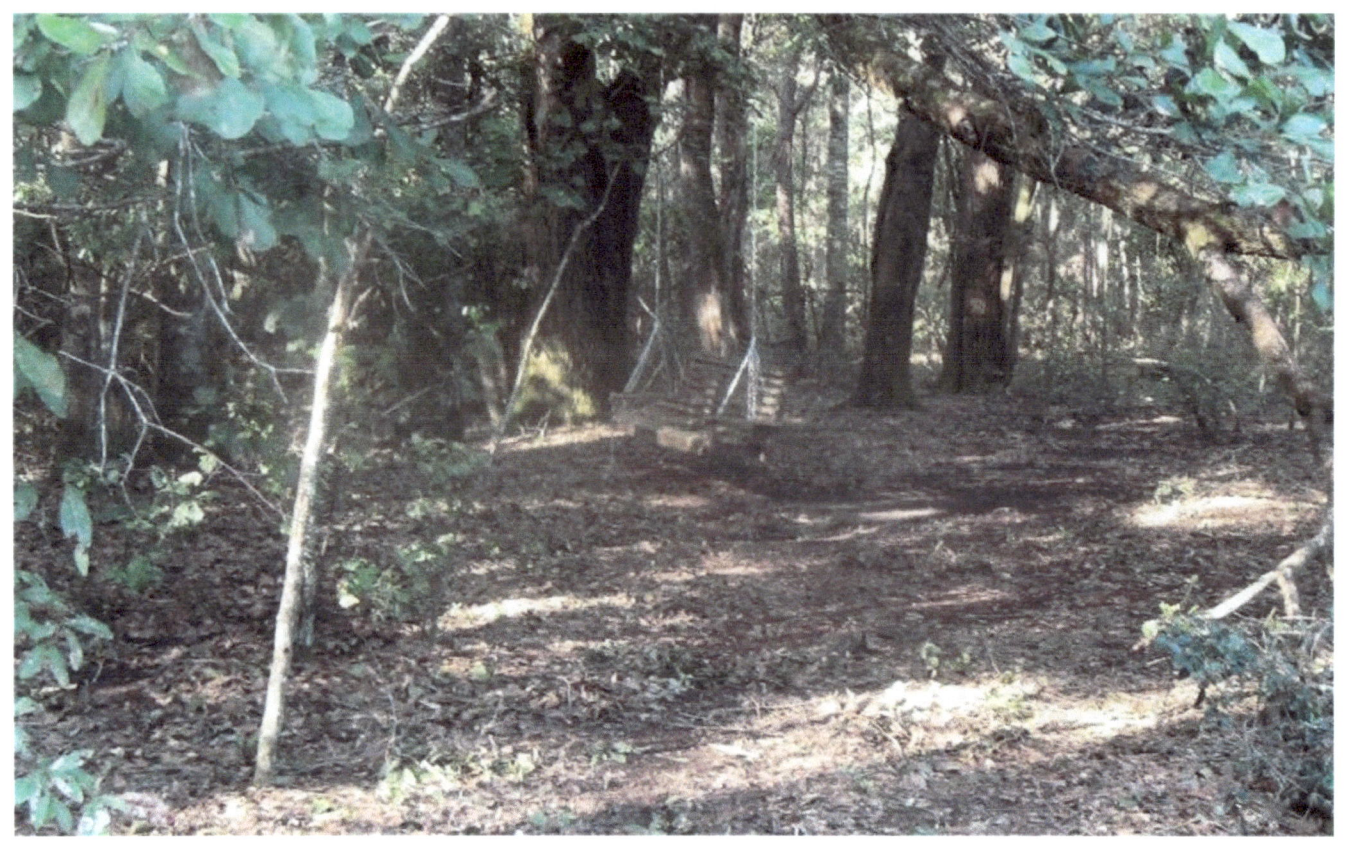

Bower Swing – Bark and limbs drawn with too heavy a hand can overpower the image of trees and intricate branches animated by the touch of a breeze or wind.

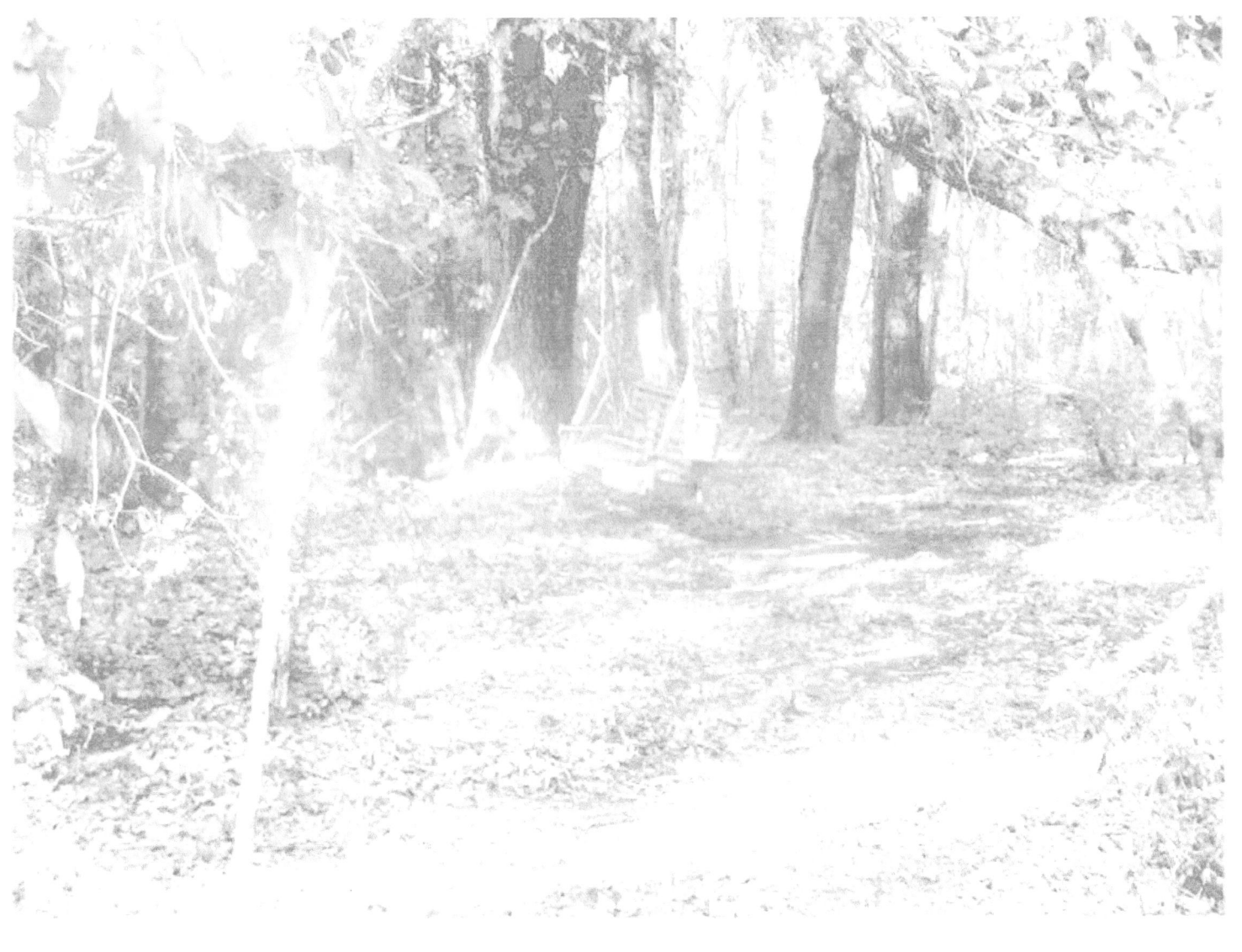

Set your imprint into the trunk of the bower's mighty oak as you enjoy a lazy "swing" beneath its soaring limbs.

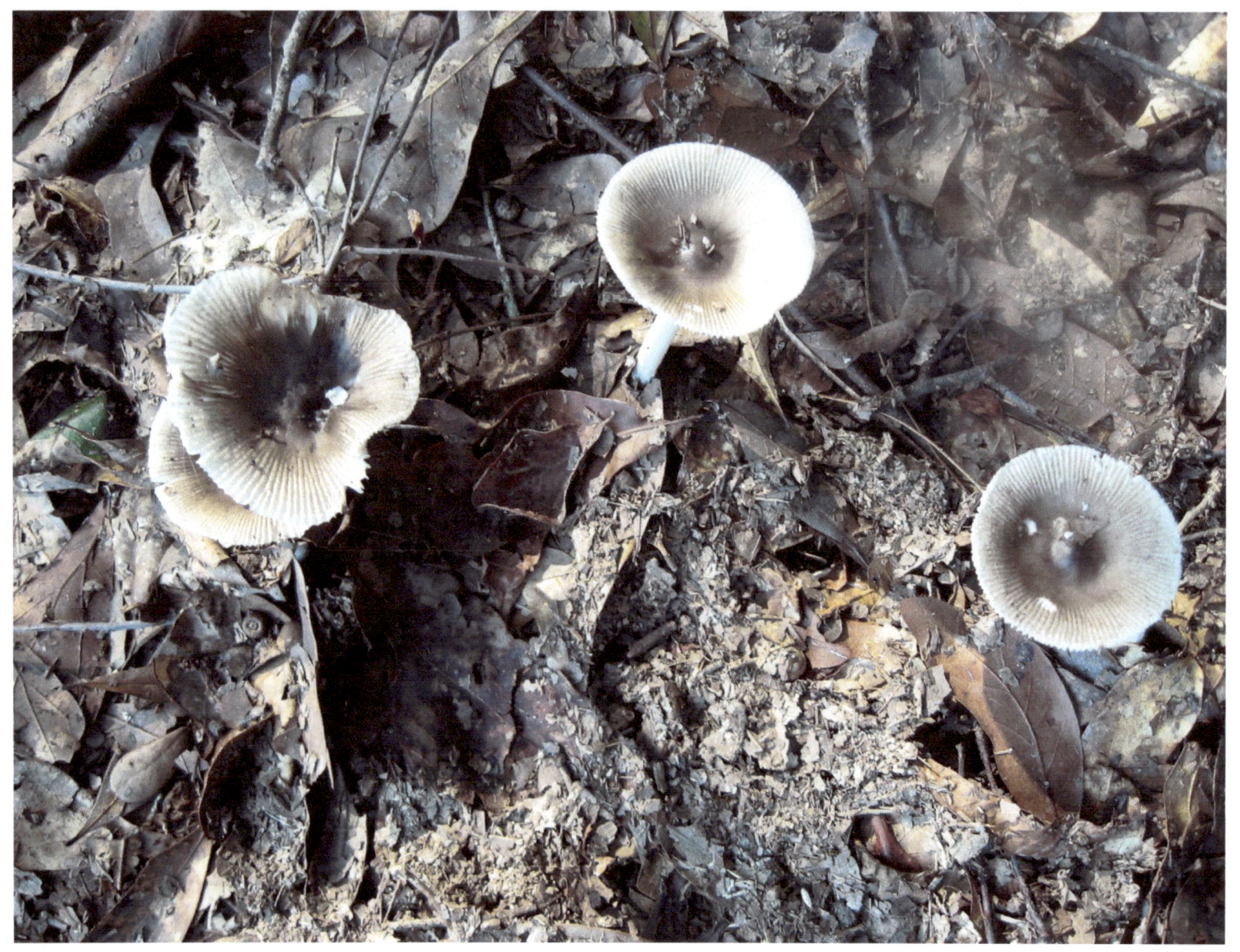

Forest floor - never barren

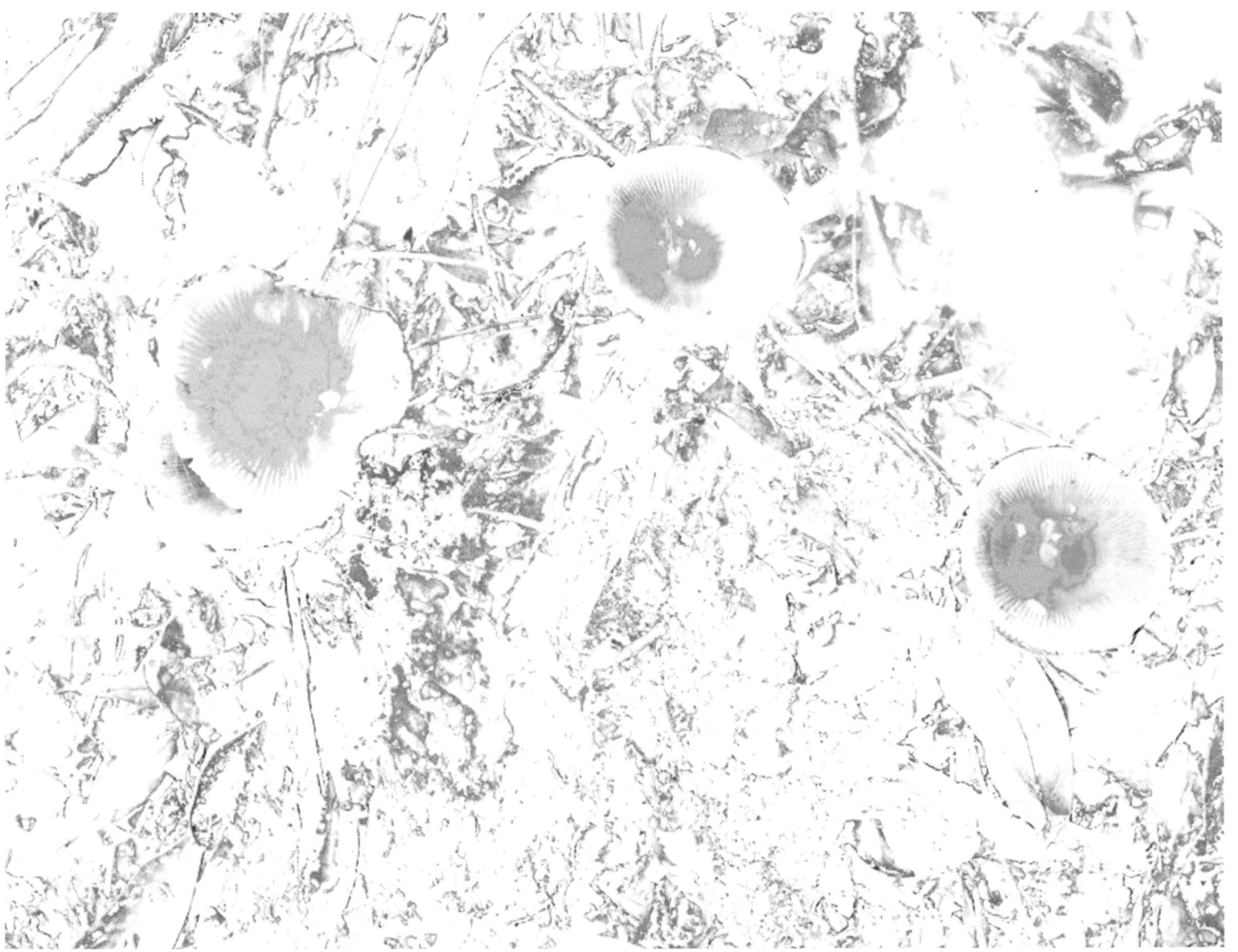

17

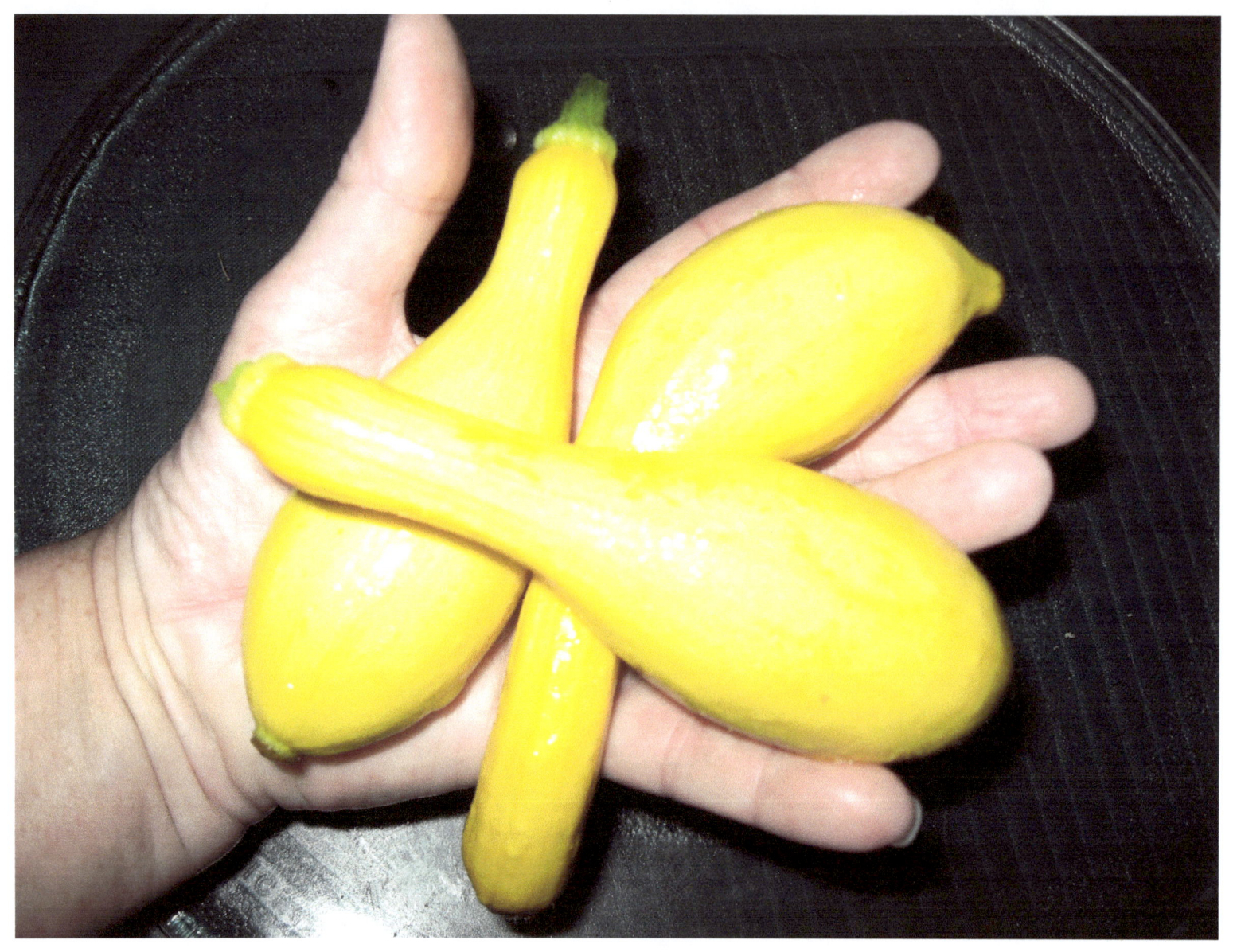

Summer's Golden Harvest

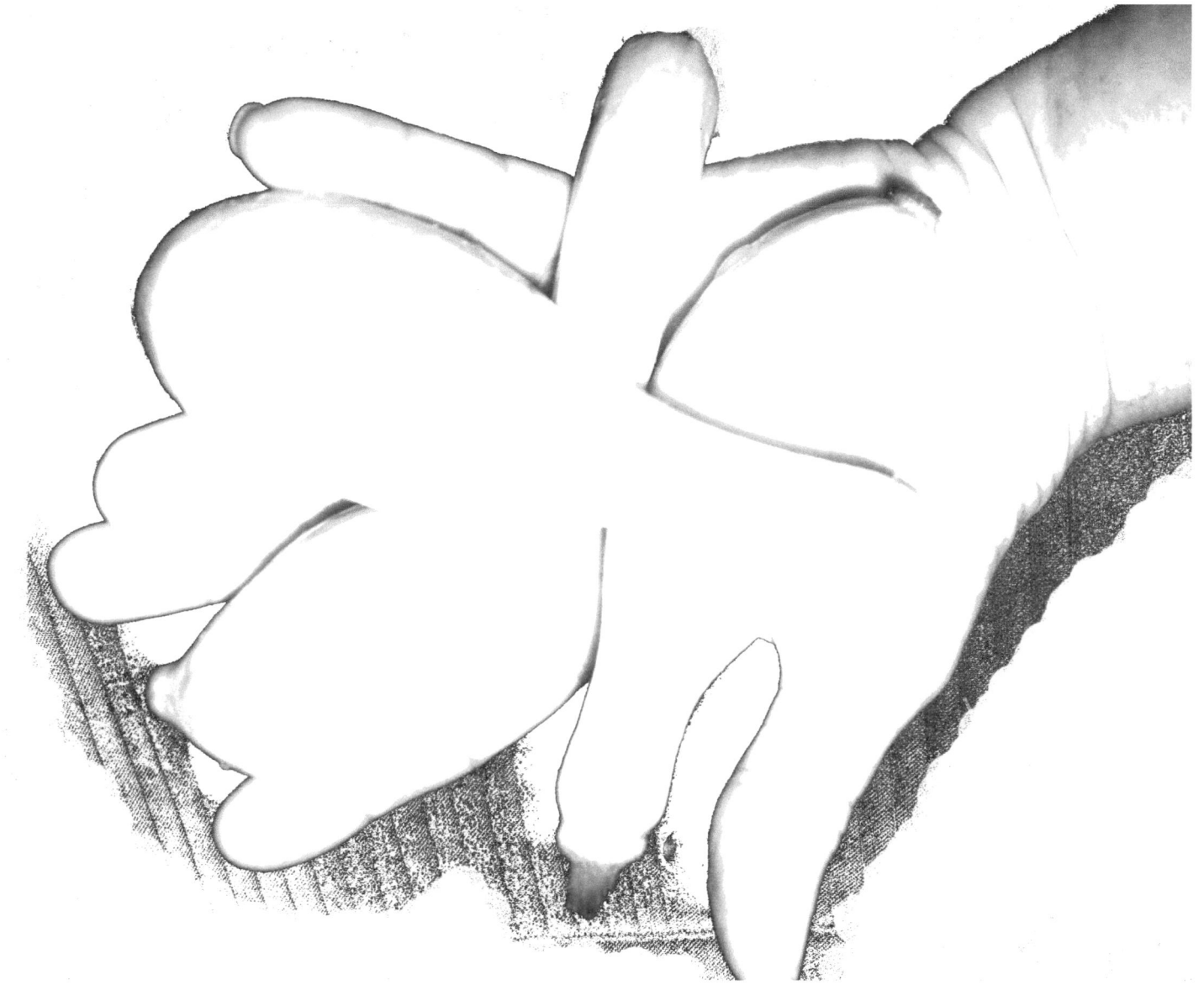

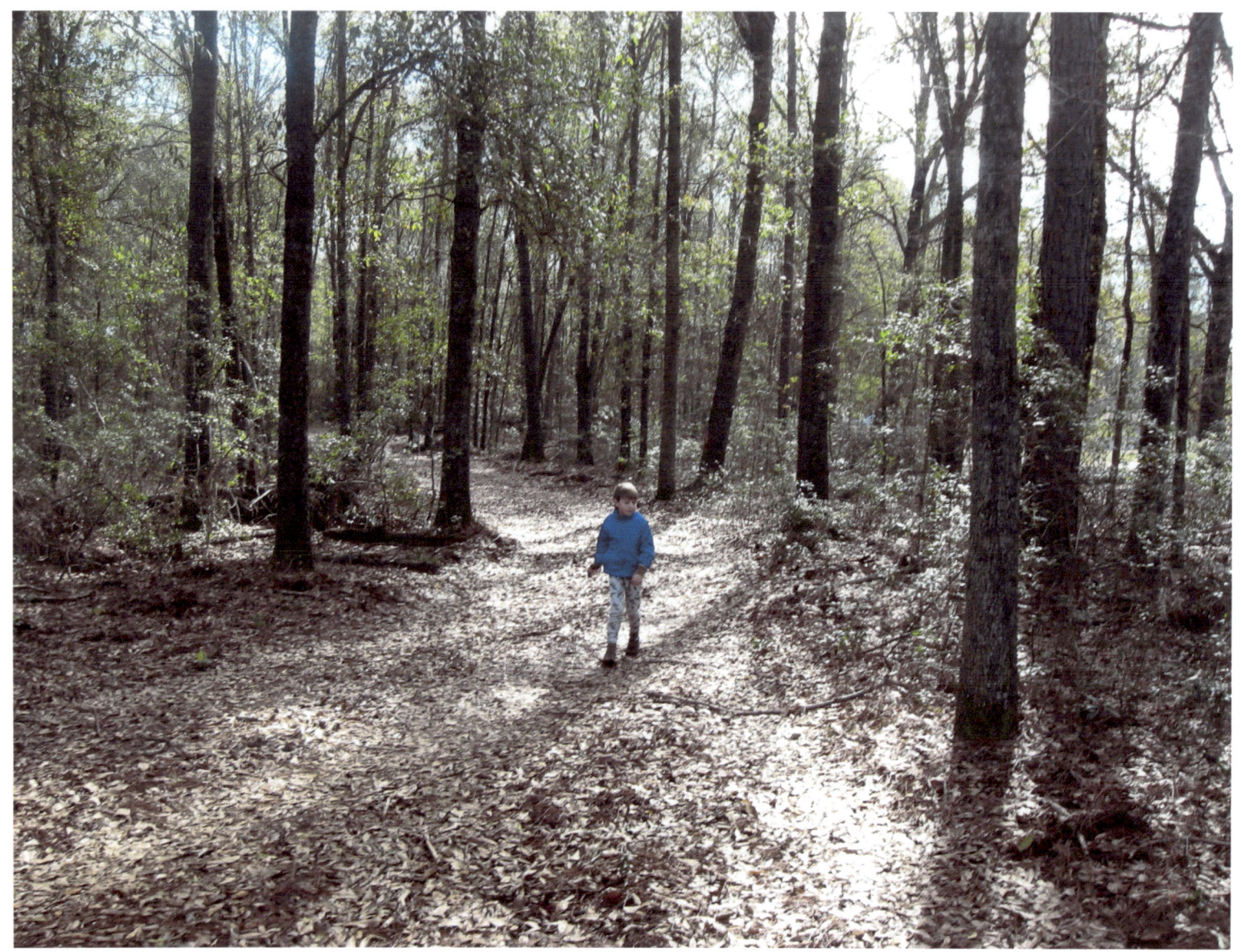

*Wooded Walk*

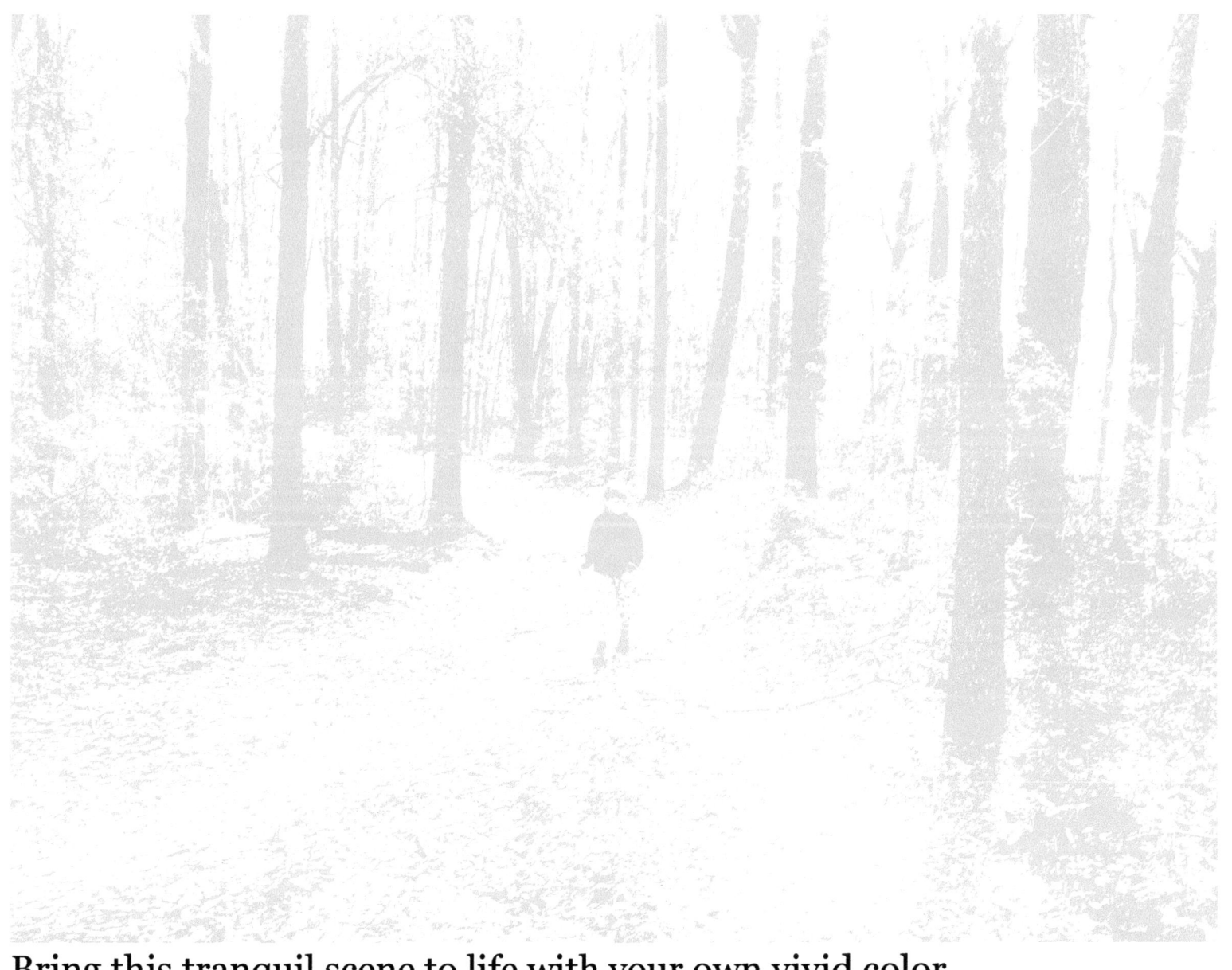

Bring this tranquil scene to life with your own vivid color.

***

Water

Vistas

Offer

a

Singular

Challenge

to

Beginning

Artists

***

When beginning a

drawing or painting

featuring a distinctive

horizon line, begin

by sketching in that

element on your

paper or canvas.

Make this line as

nearly horizontal as

possible.

Realism in water color
can often be achieved by
employing the
*absence*
of color in your artwork.

Conversely,
the motion of waves
or streams
can be shown
using deep shades
and dark highlights.

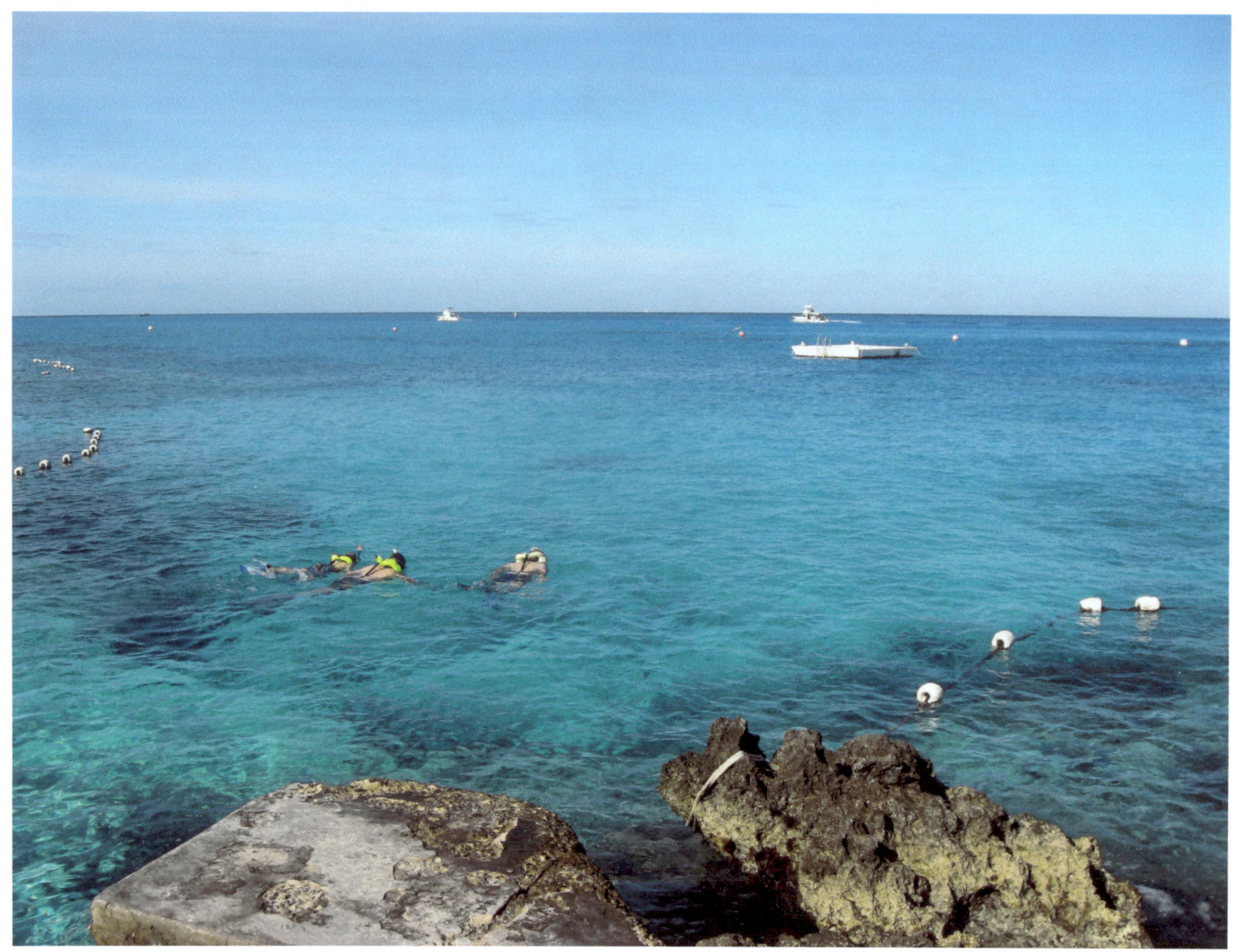

Cozumel Snorkelers

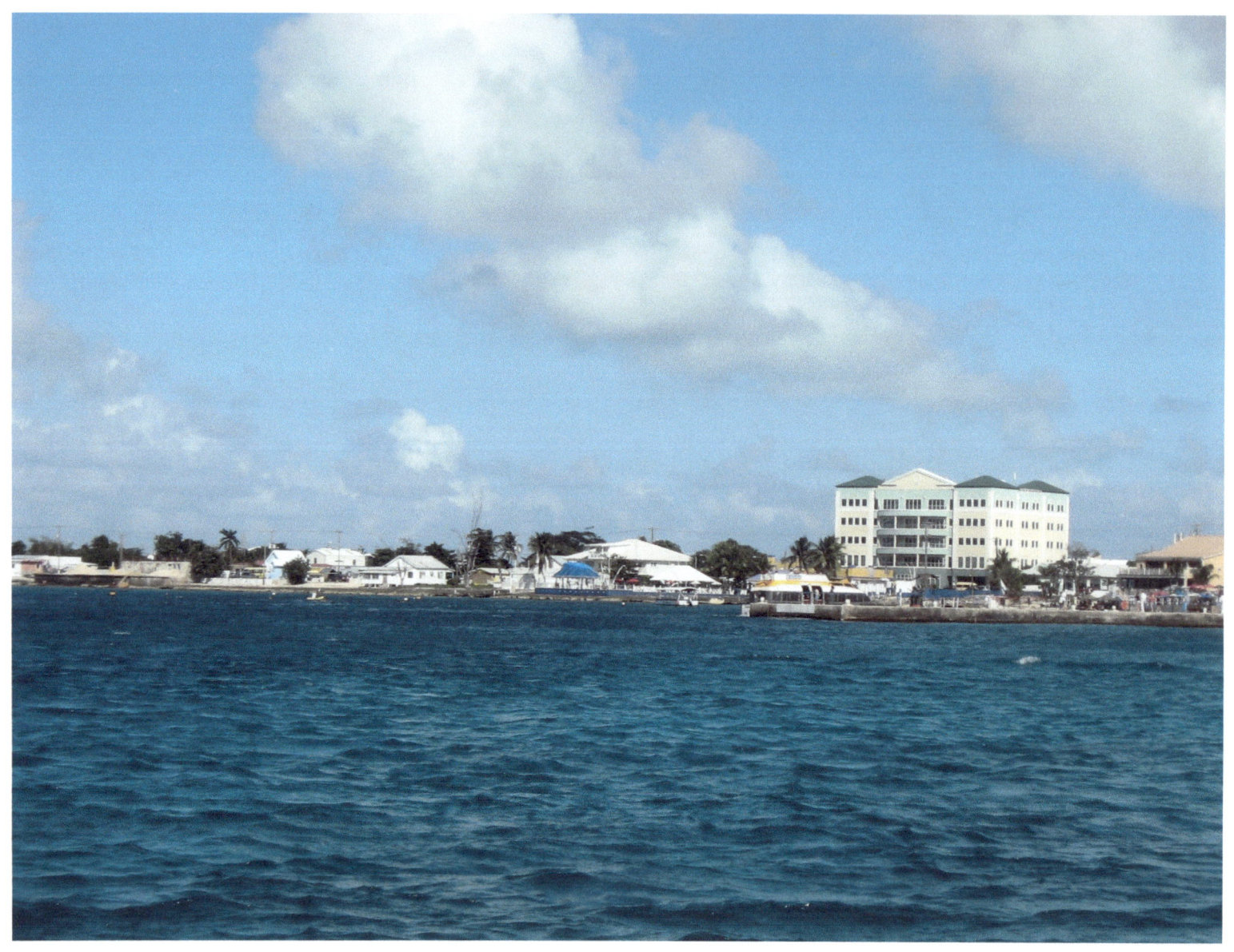

Grand Cayman in Azure

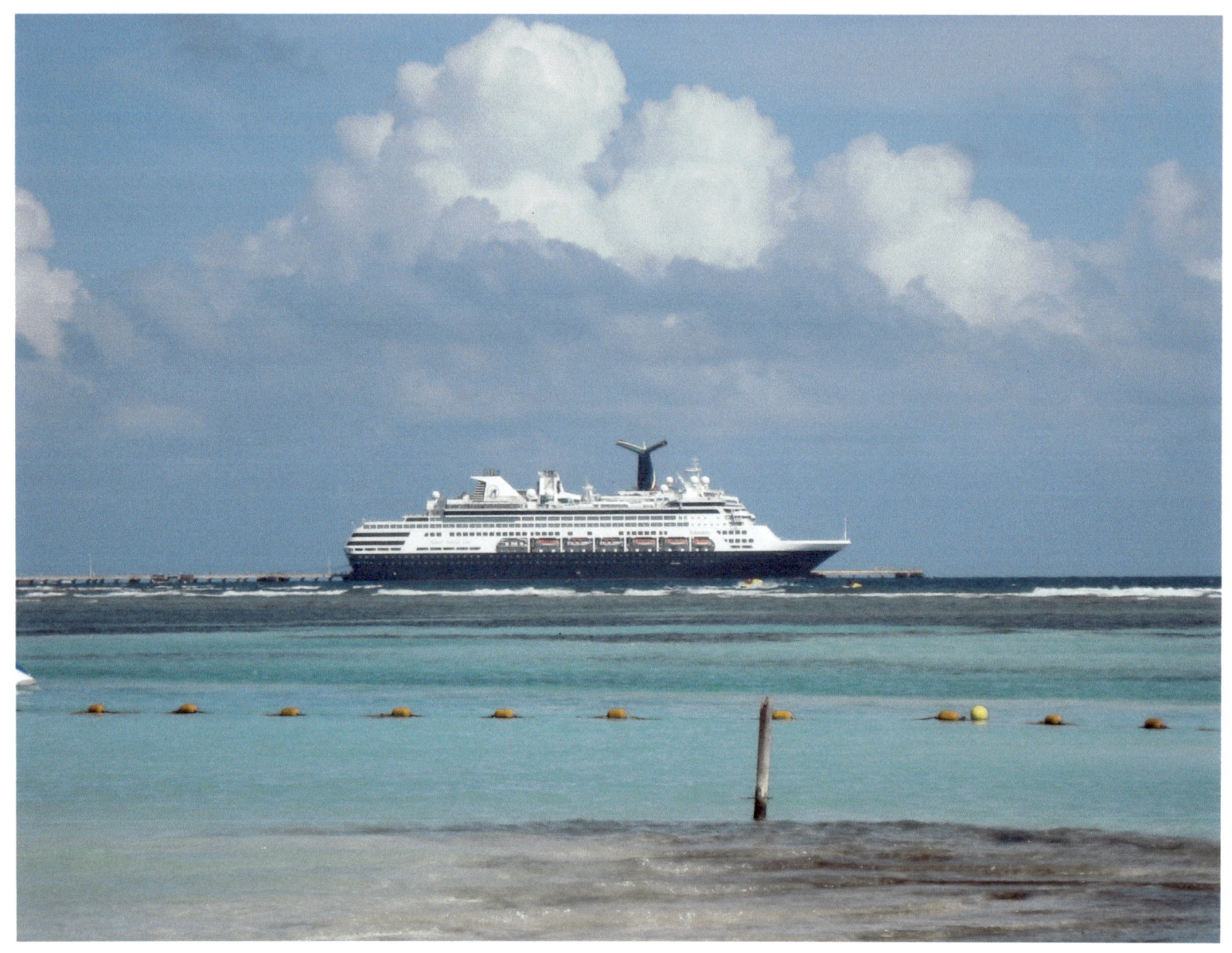

Distant Cruiser

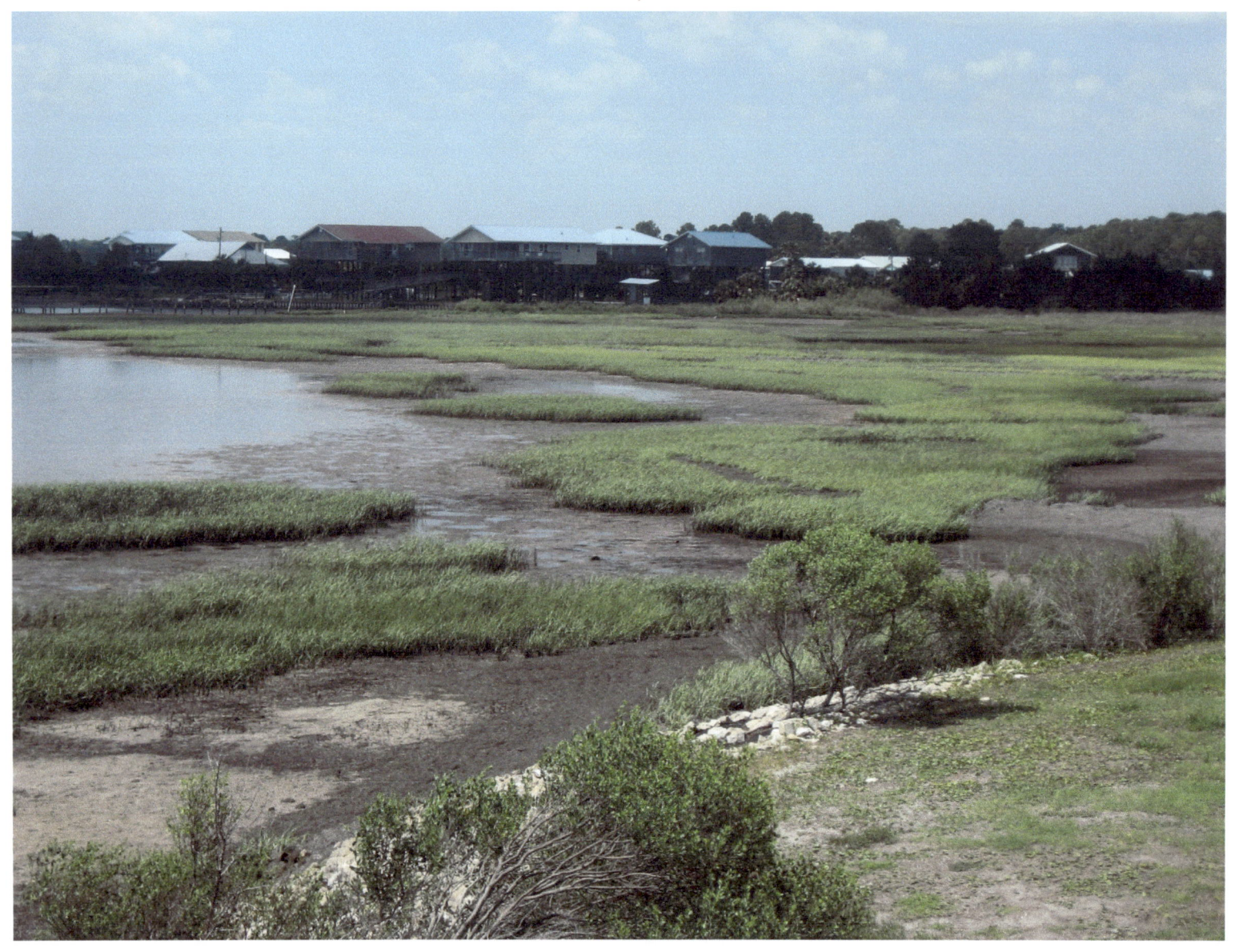

Coastal Plain

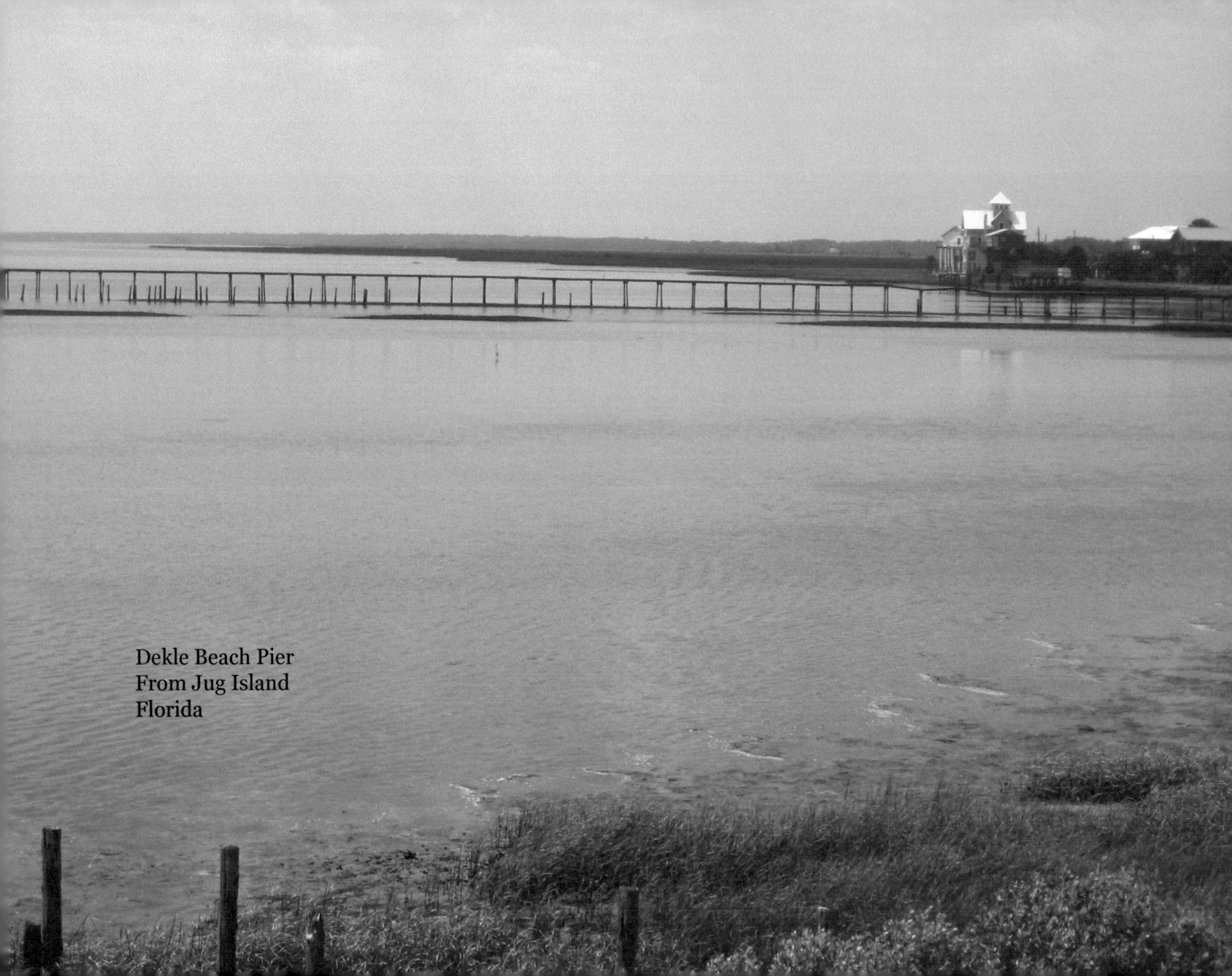

Dekle Beach Pier
From Jug Island
Florida

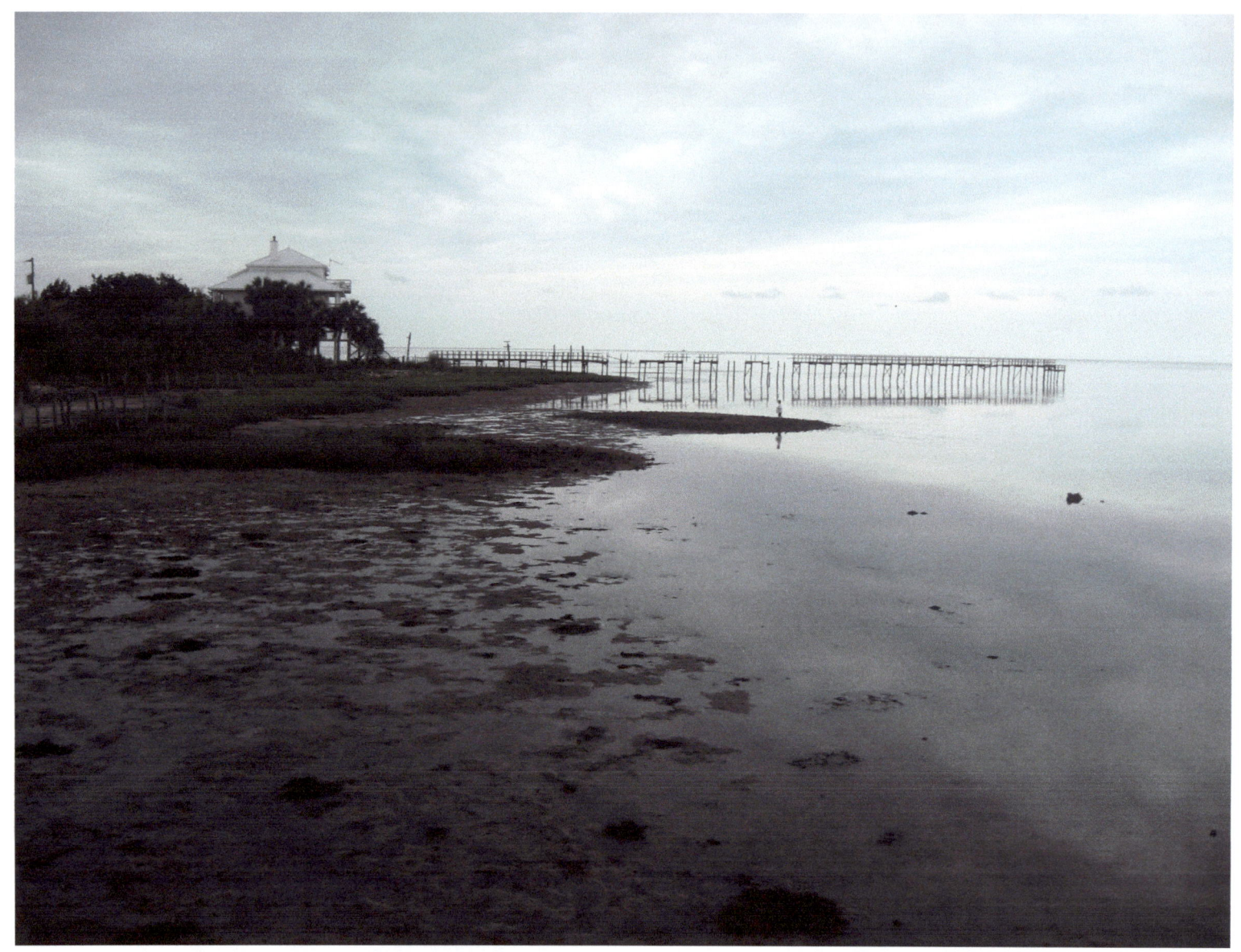

Aging Timbers, Jug Island Florida

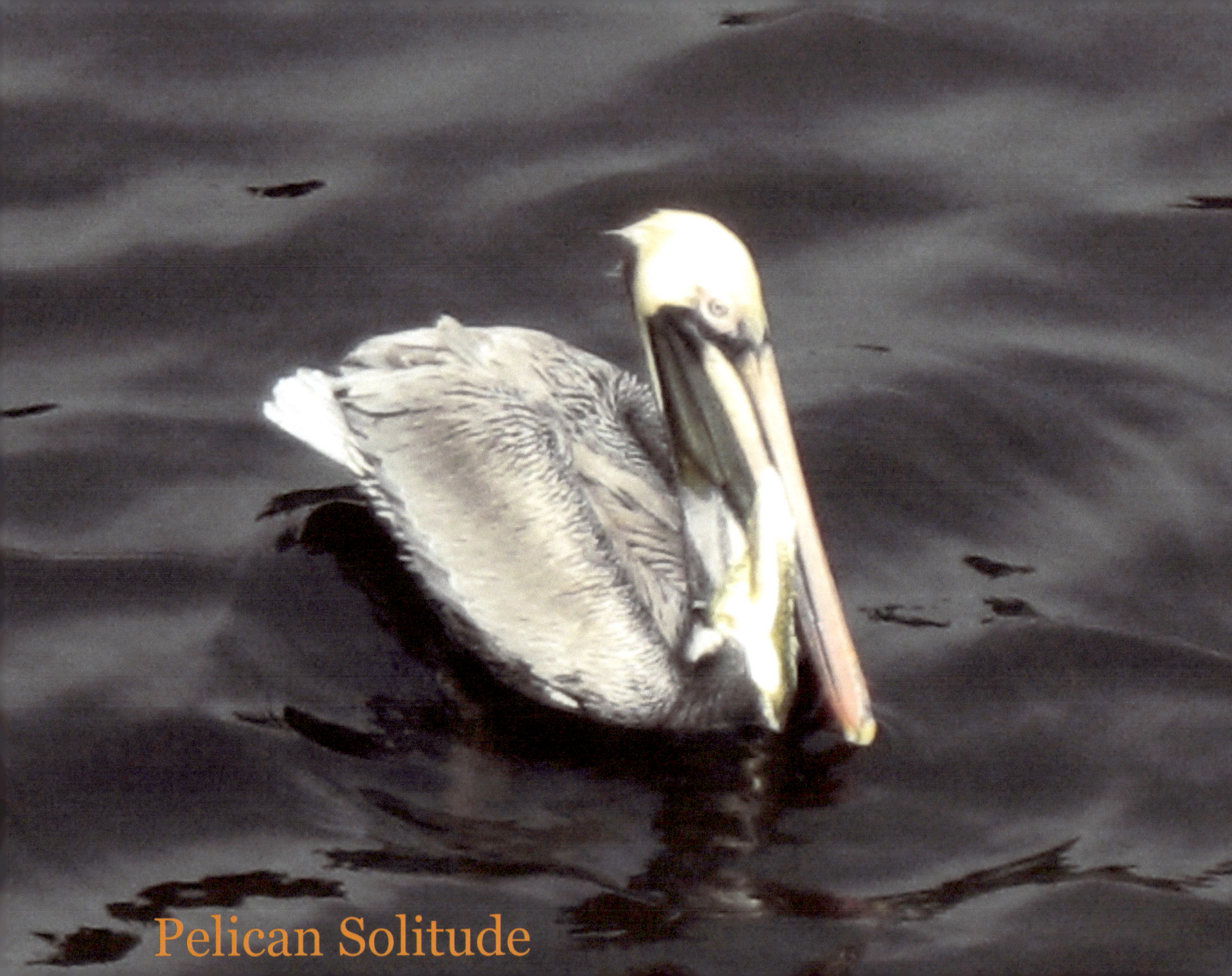

Pelican Solitude

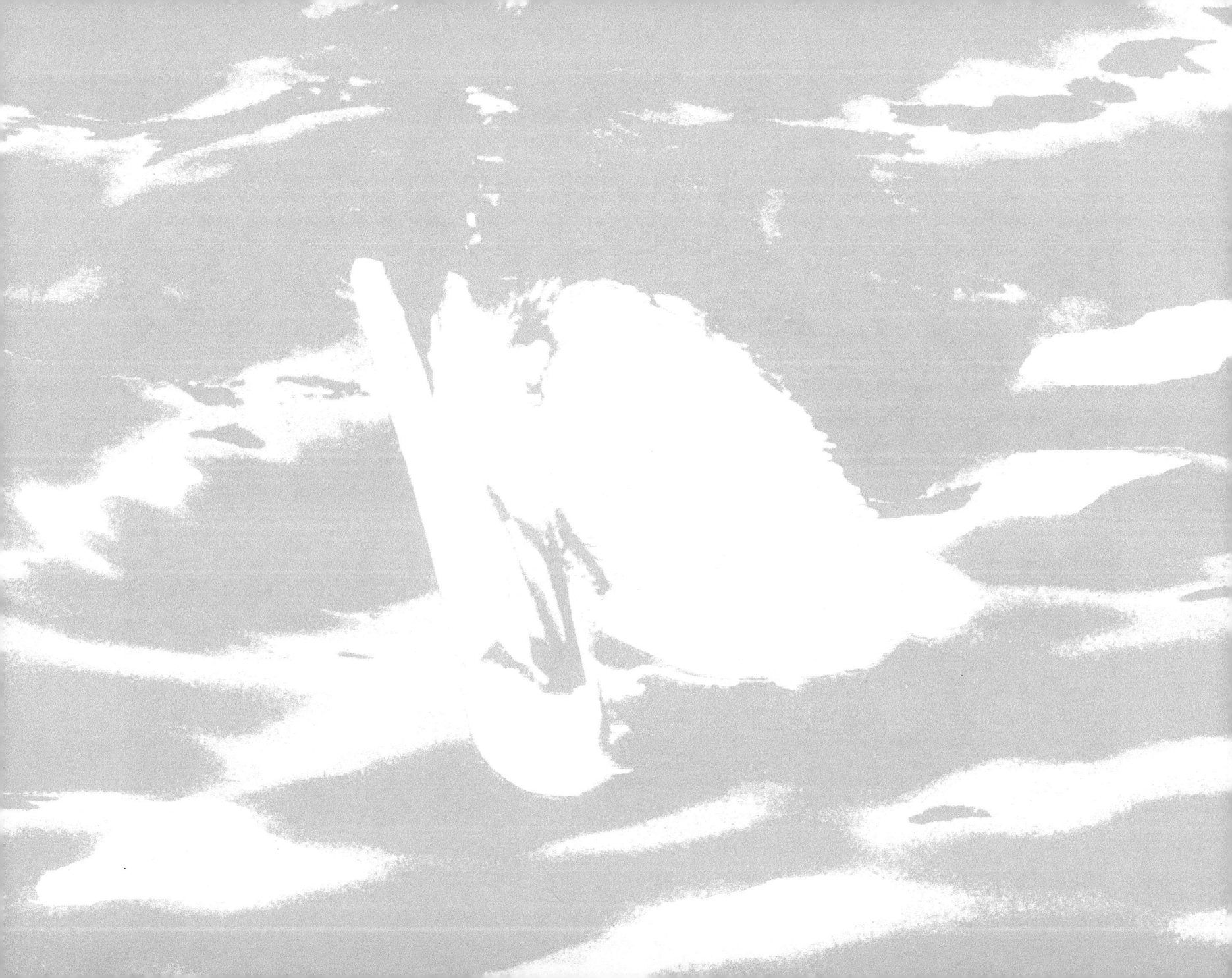

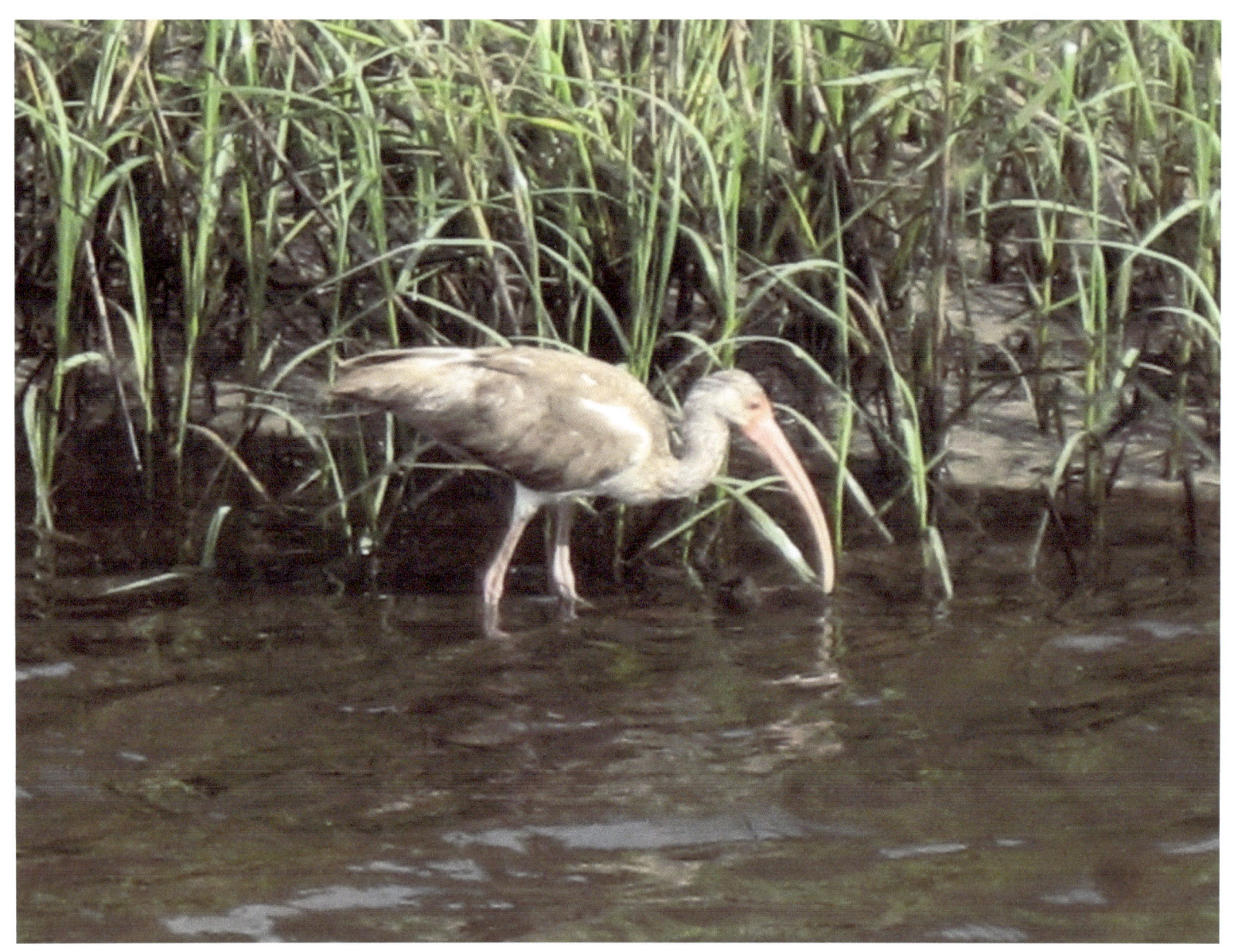

Marshy Browser

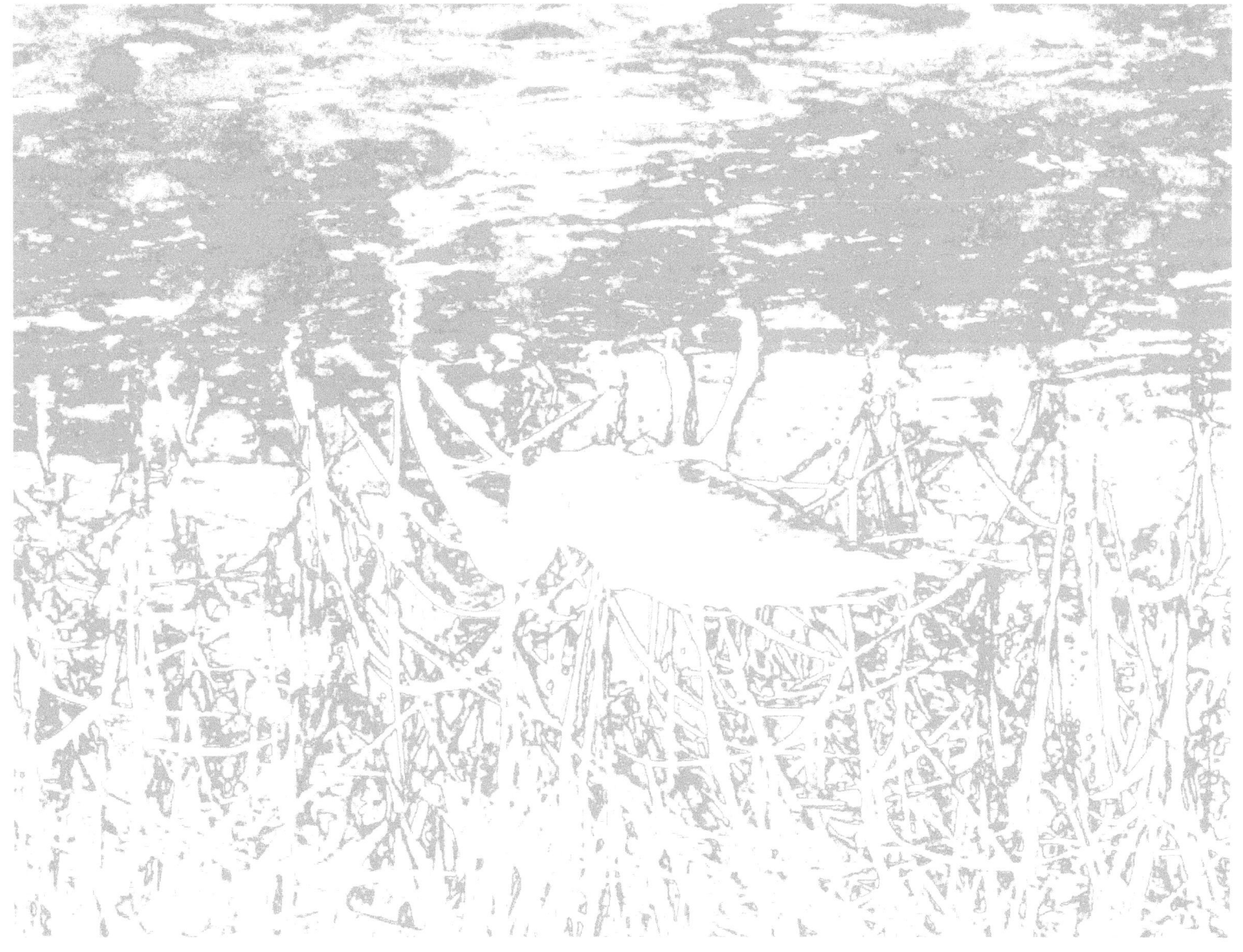

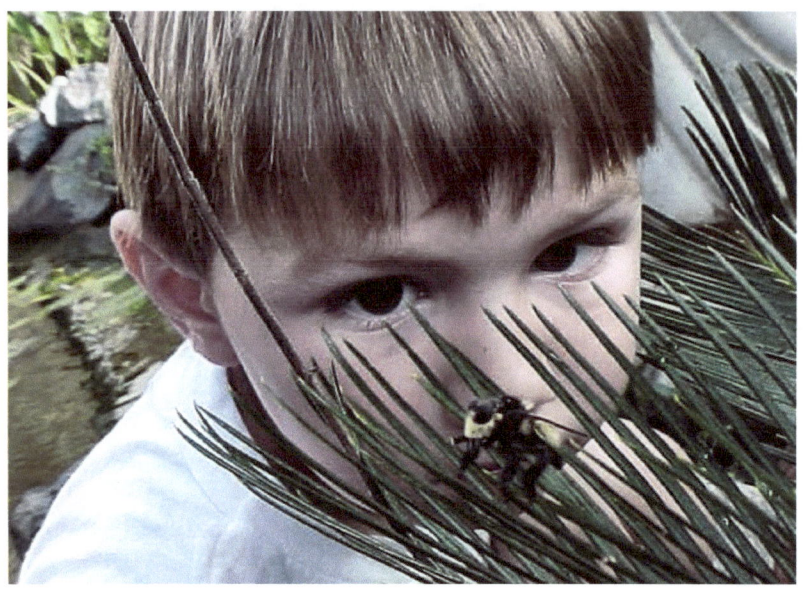

Muted Conversation

Some say that faithful representation of the **_human face_** proves the mettle of an artist.

This selection offers a double challenge in the poignant image of a child immersed in unspoken communication with a resting hornet.

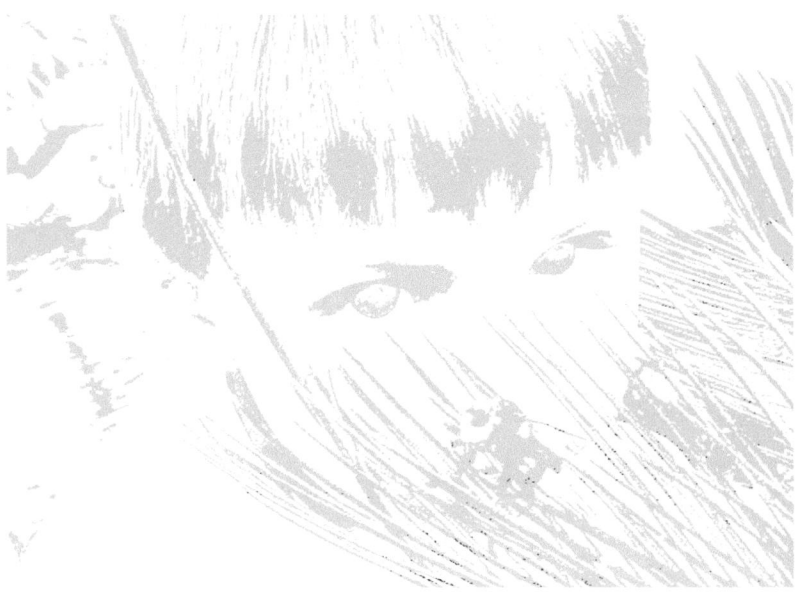

Light and shadow play
across hair and eyes,
bringing warmth and
vibrancy to both human
and insect.

Apply pen or paint
with a soft touch
to hair and lashes,
insect wings and
fronds of grass.

Use rich hues to
deepen eye color,
with mere hints of
reflected light.

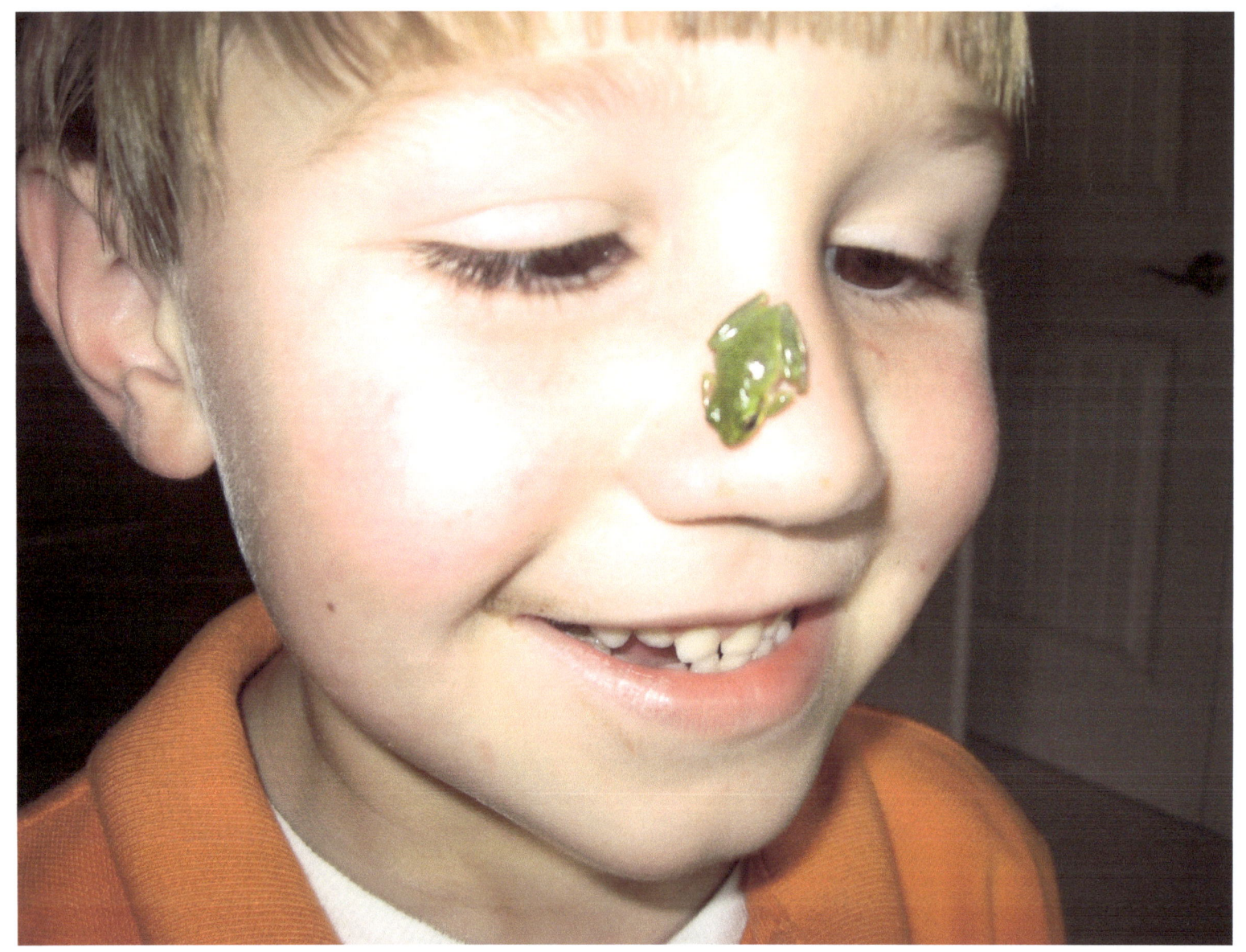

Nosey Neighbor

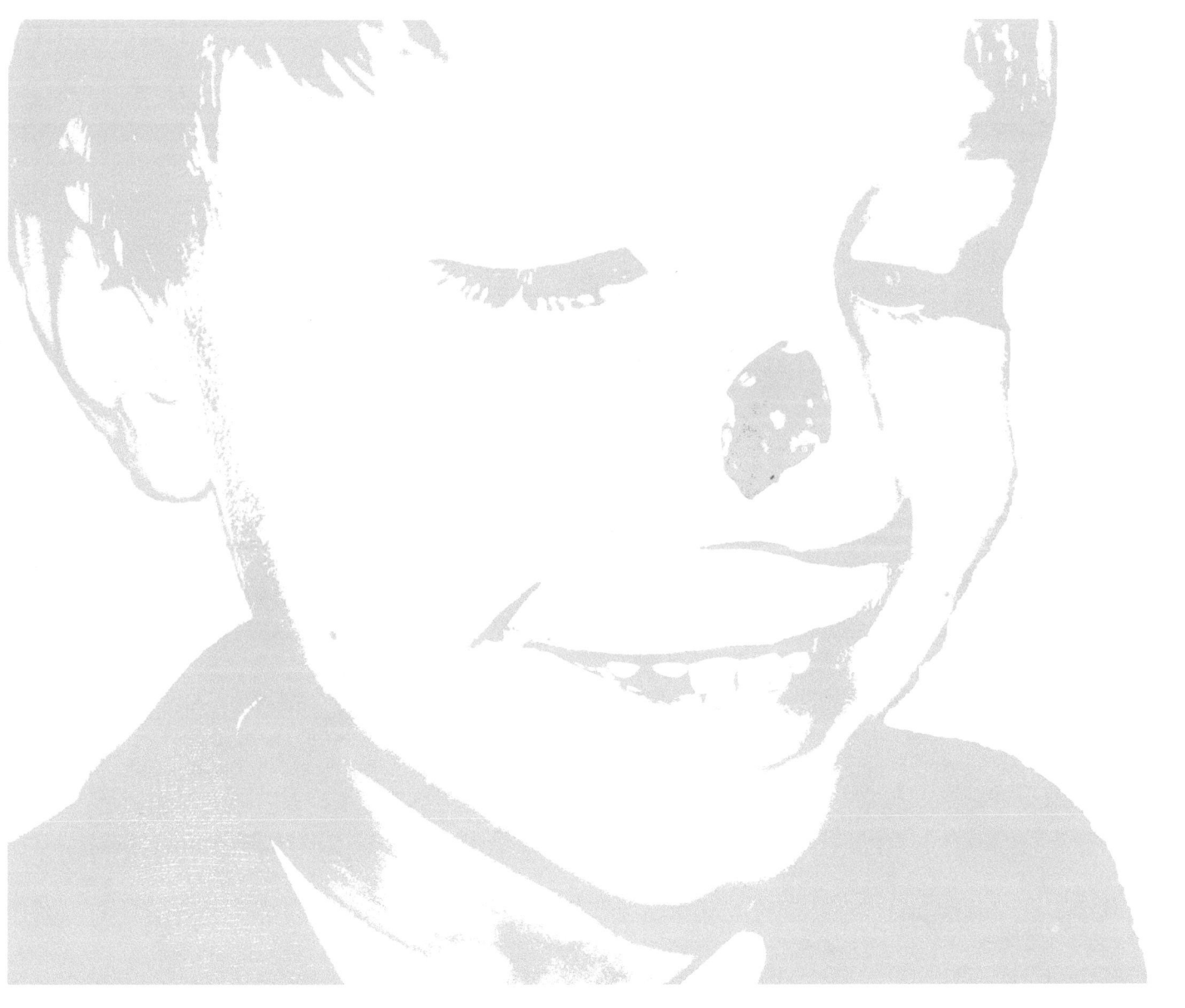

Use subtlety when blending flesh tones; yet flamboyance for the greens of the frog.

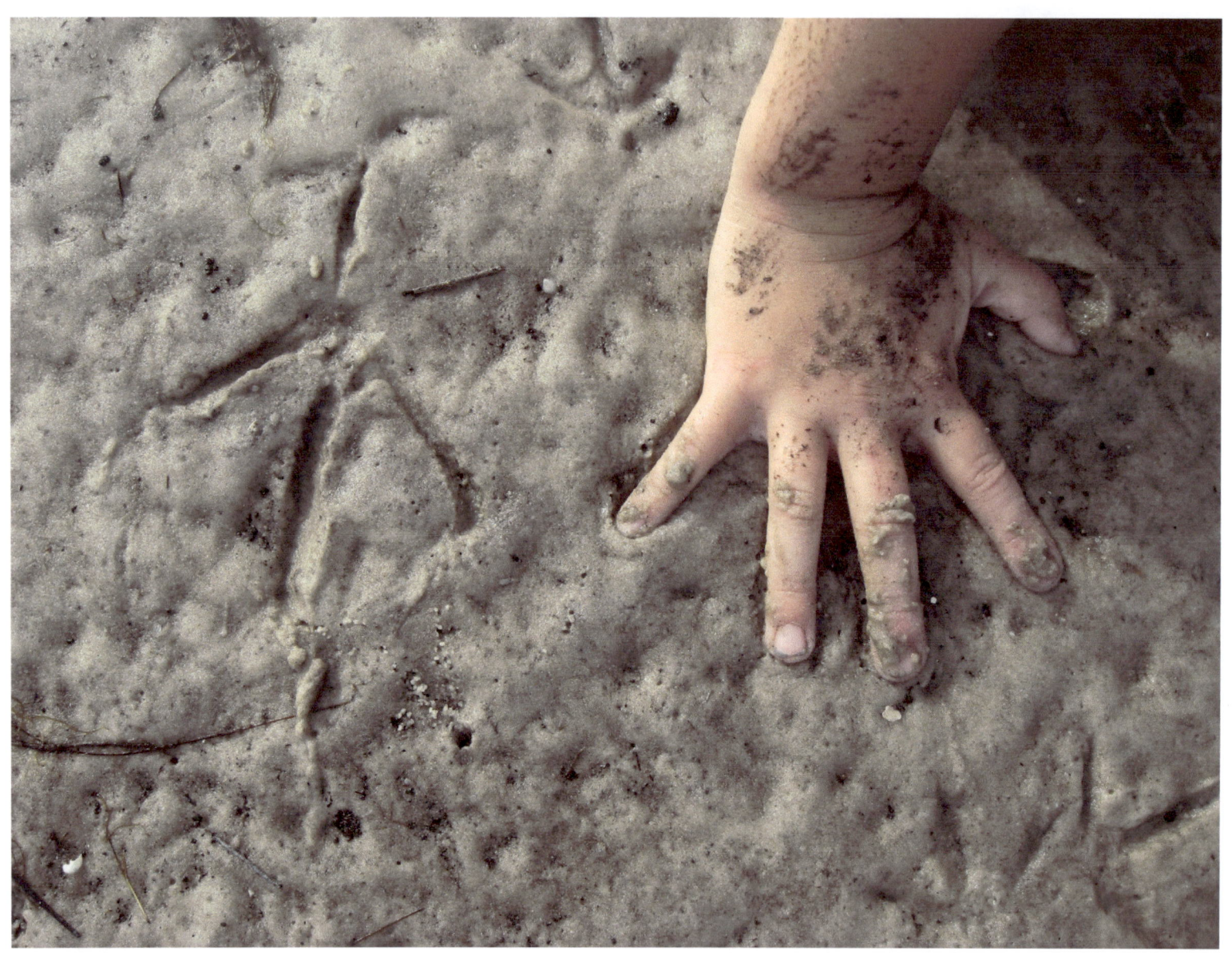

Sandprints.......
Before the turning of the tide.......

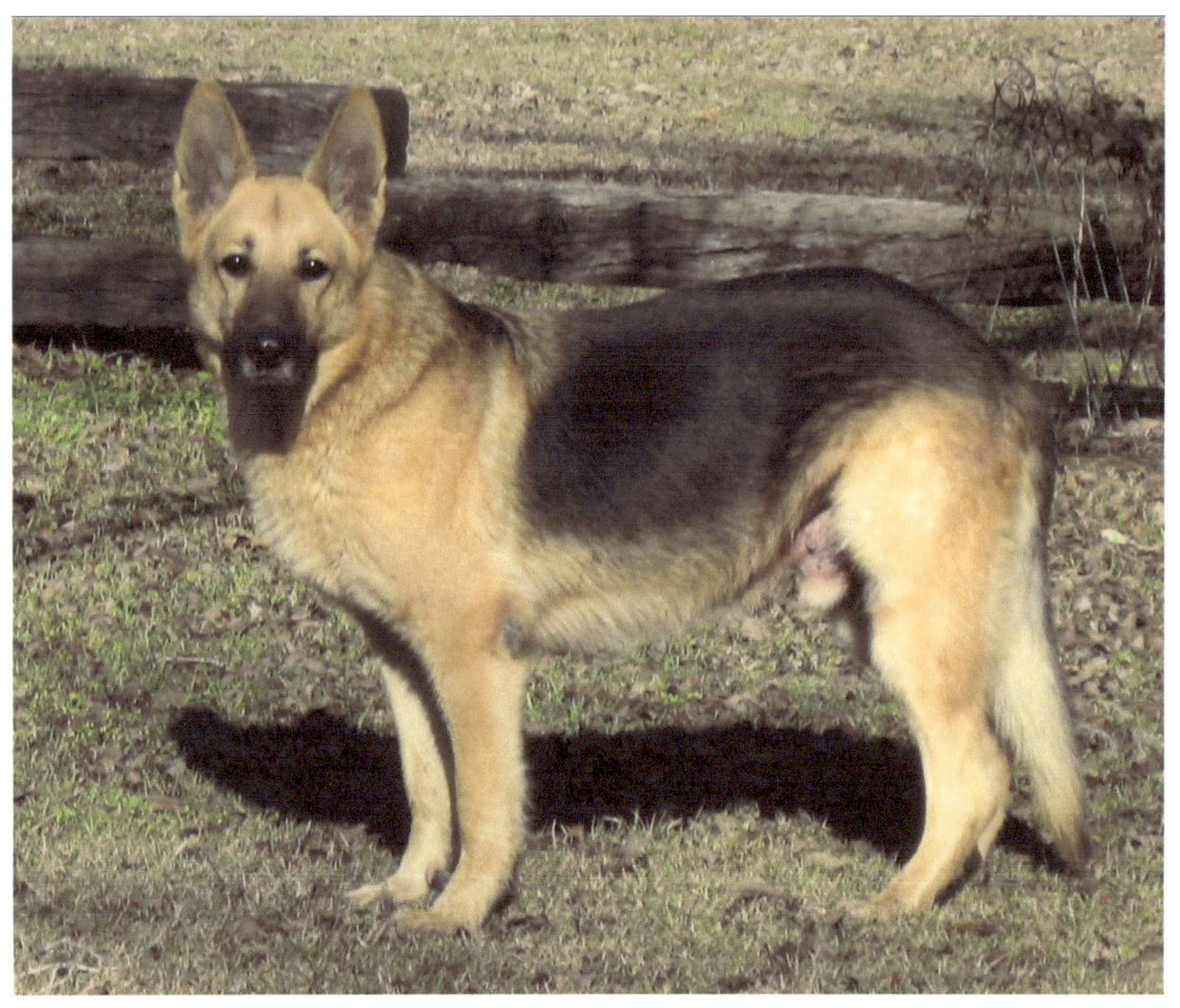

Shiloh Noir Majesty – Beloved Companion Immortalized in Print

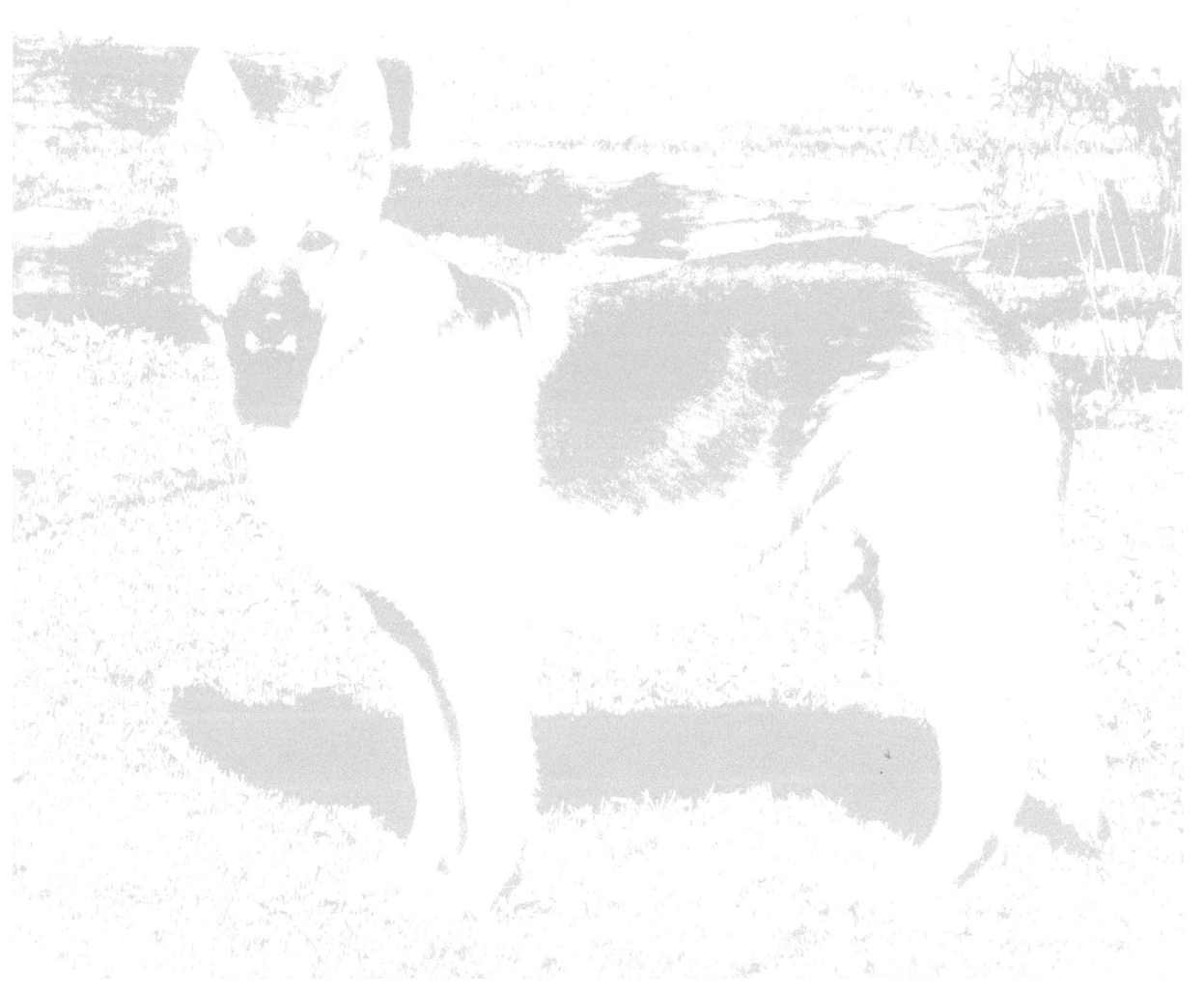

Allow your colors to point up the light reflected from fathomless eyes and gleaming coat.
Use finely sharpened colored pencils or feathery brushes to achieve life-like details.

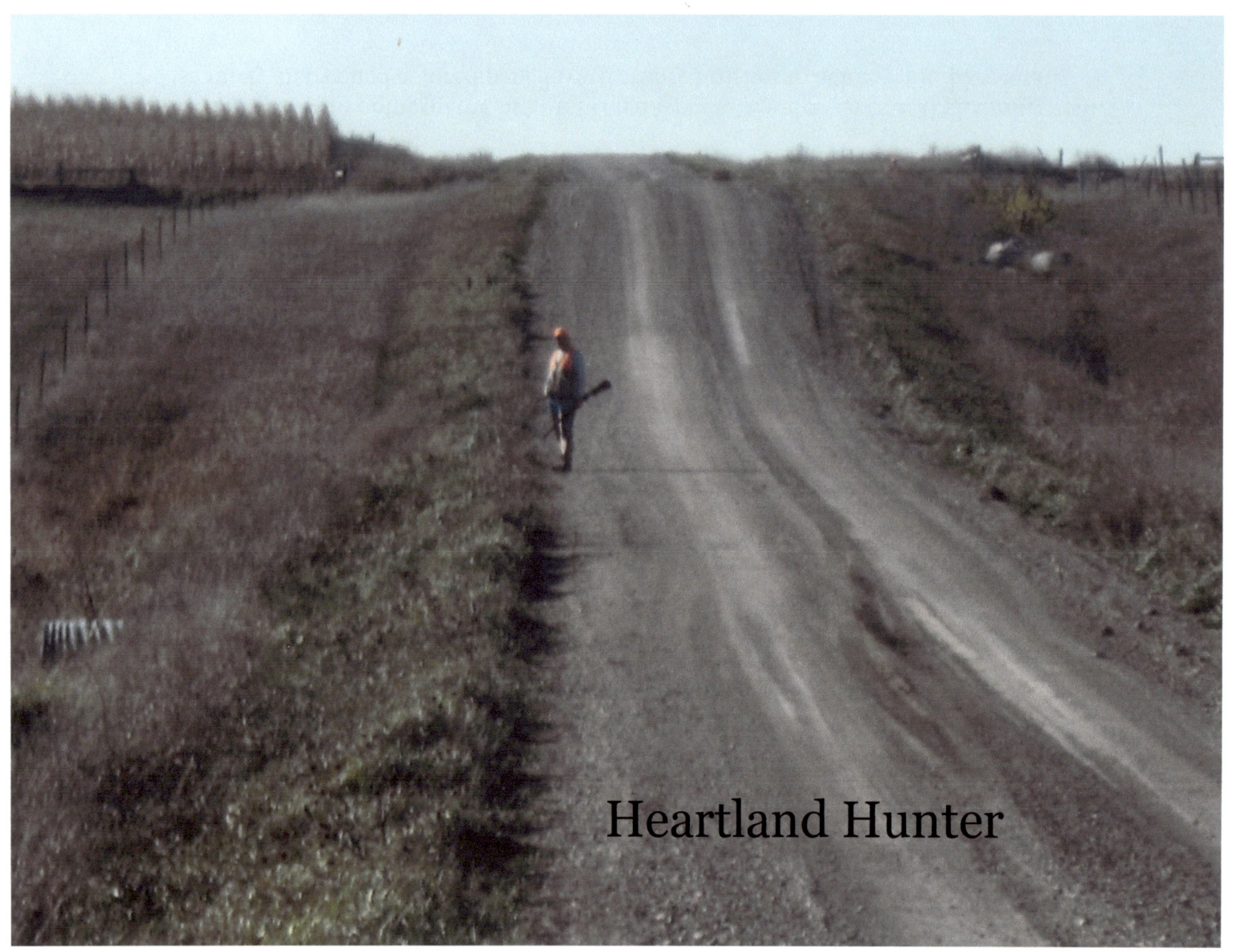

Heartland Hunter

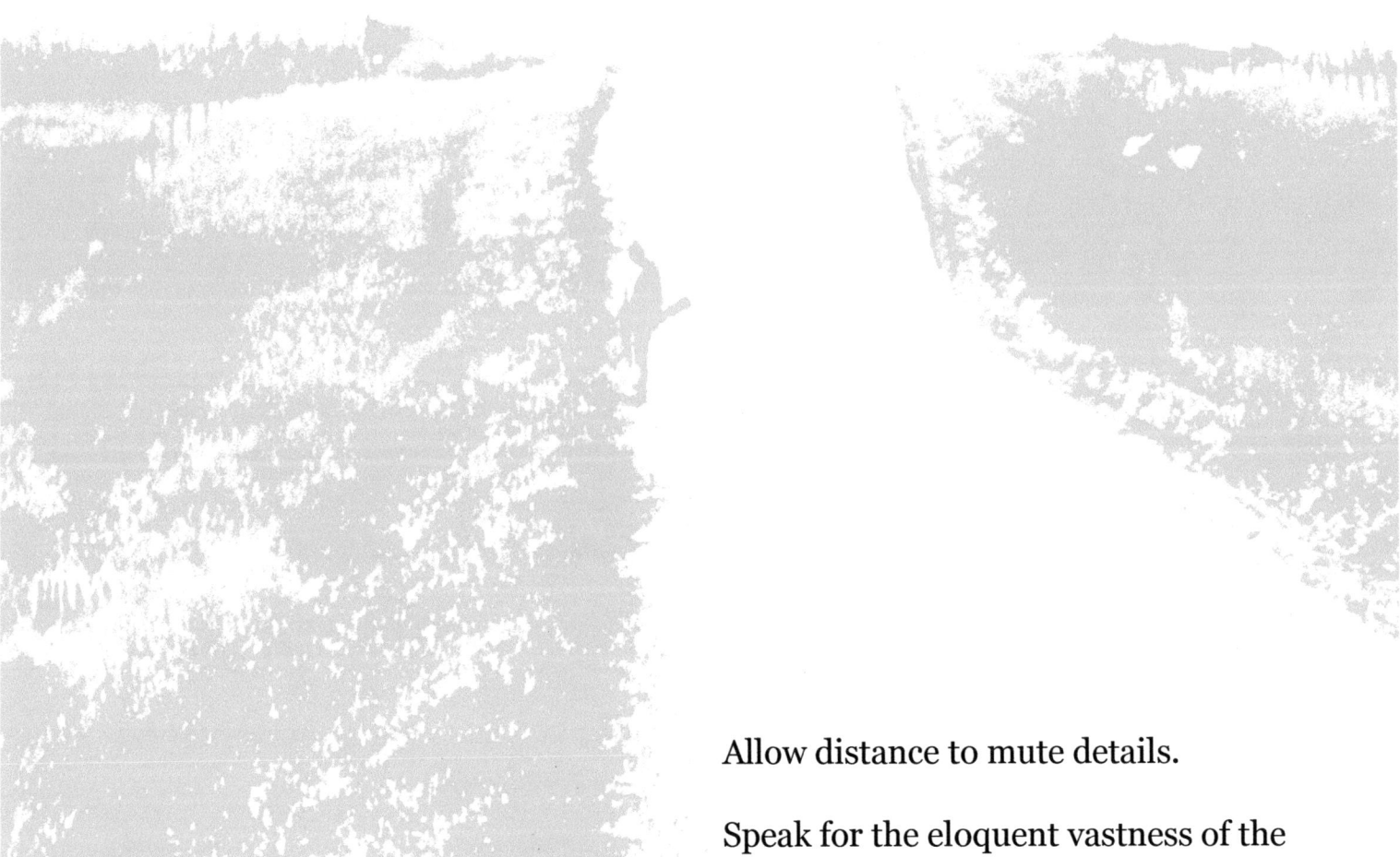

Allow distance to mute details.

Speak for the eloquent vastness of the
landscape with fields in gentle motion,
autumn's colors, incomparable solitude.

Add to your portfolio of landscapes and other traditional subjects

a few that are

a bit more whimsical.

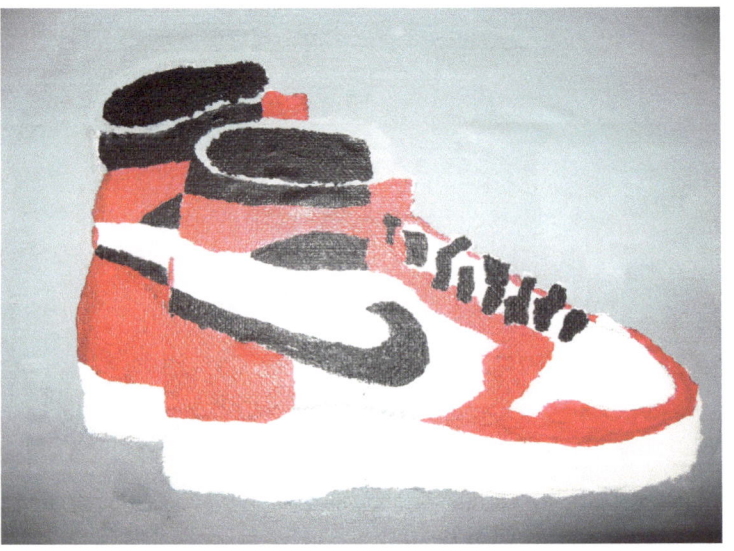

A child's favorite shoes, too special to give up


***"Still life"*** might make you think of fruit carefully arranged in a pottery bowl.

But, random items found in everyday life can contribute their own brand of artistic simplicity and visual appeal.

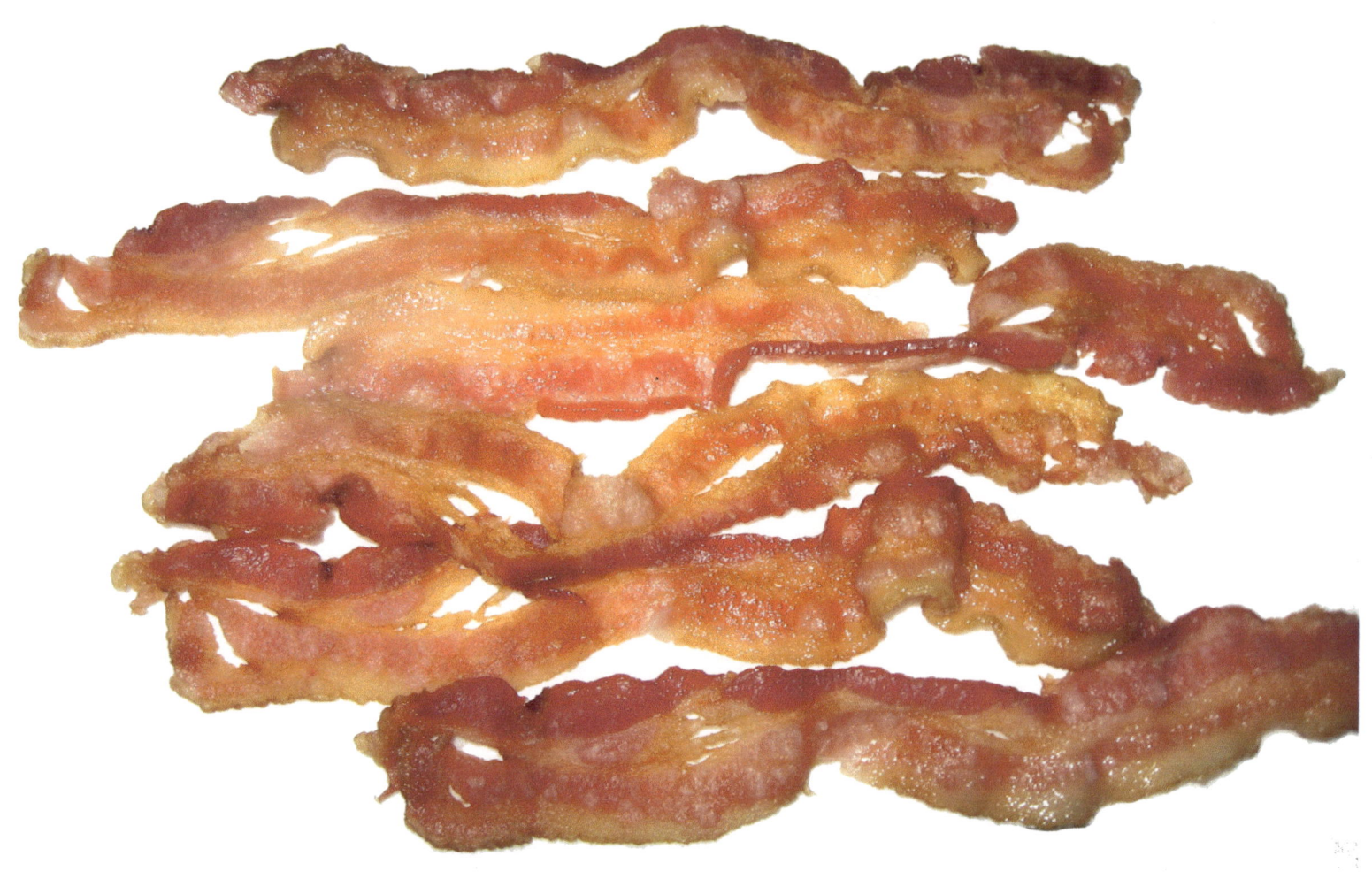

Can you almost smell the bacon?

"Fry up" these unappetizing strips to mouth watering succulence!

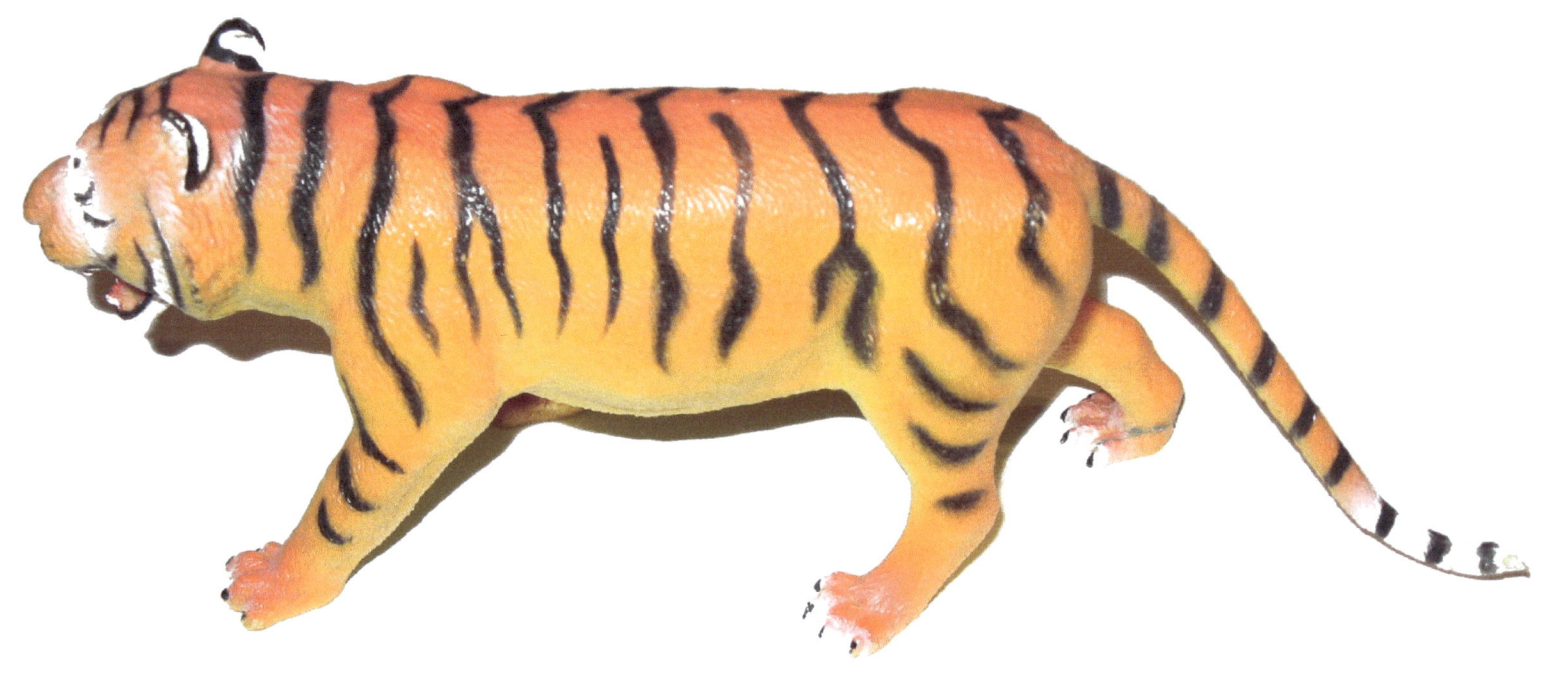

What young-at-heart artist might
enjoy this toy tiger on the prowl?

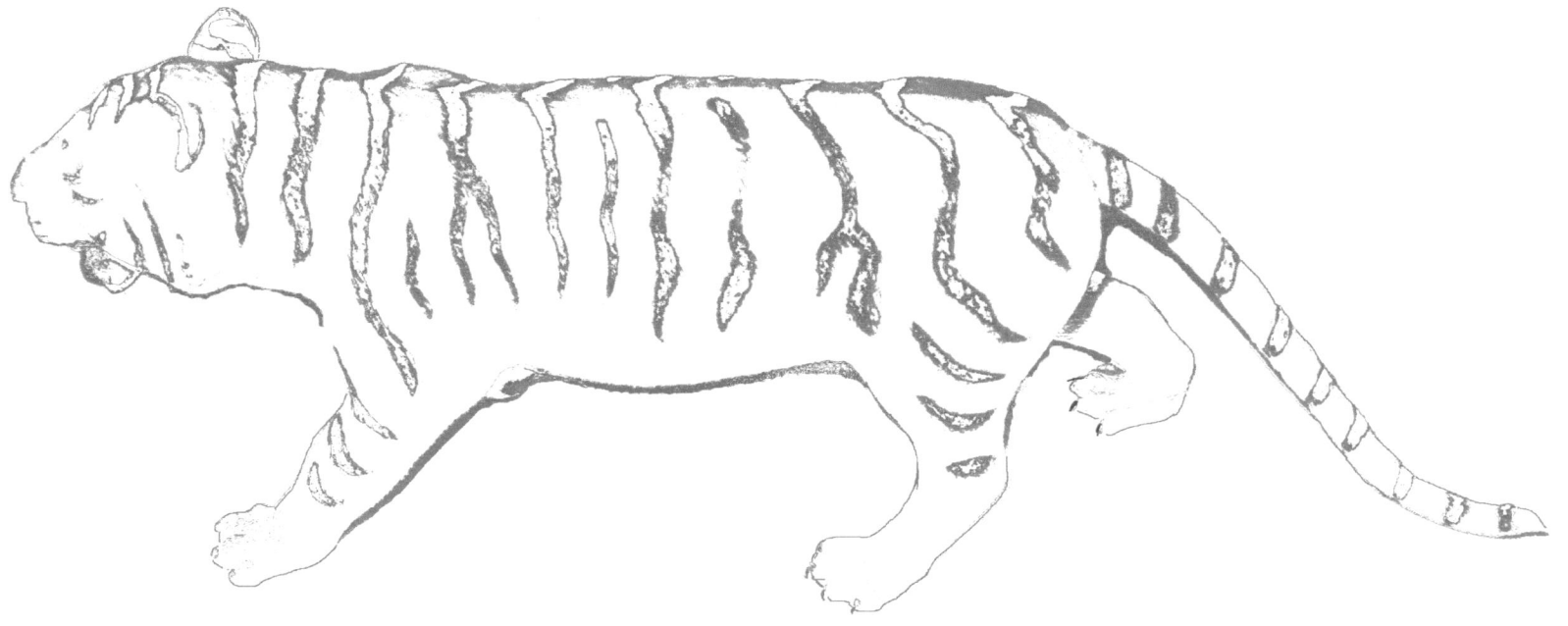

Bring him to "life" with your palette
of oranges and blacks.

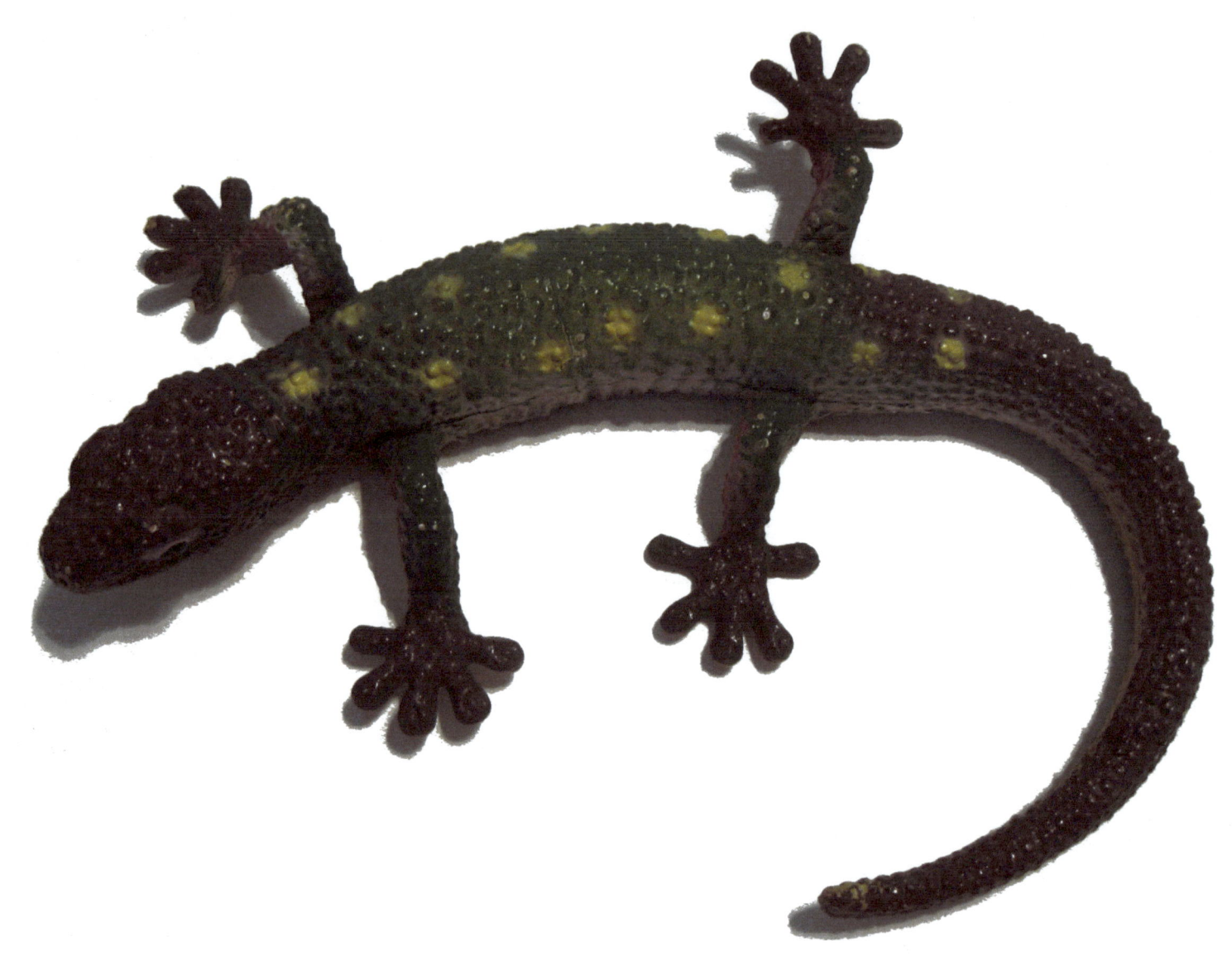

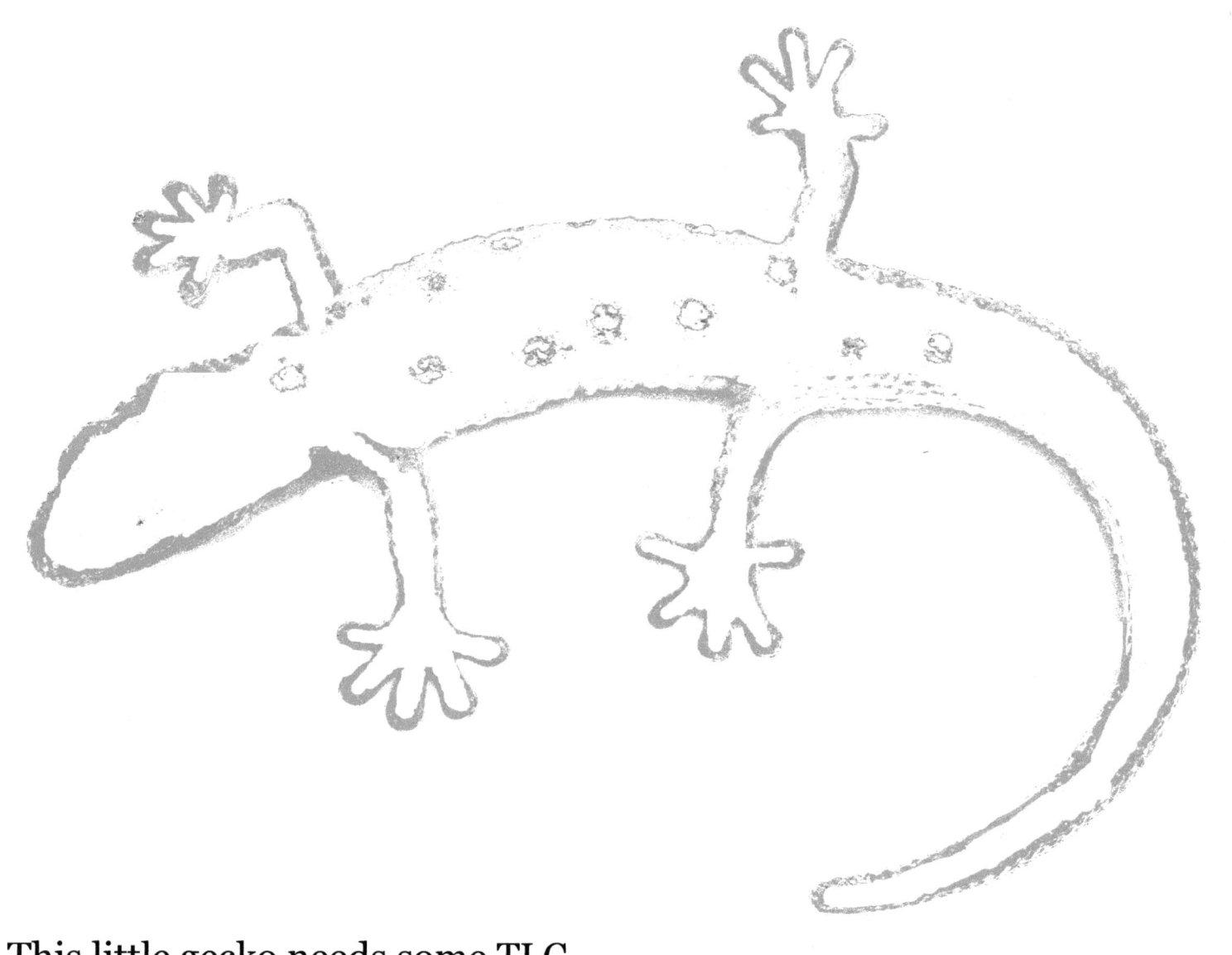

This little gecko needs some TLC.

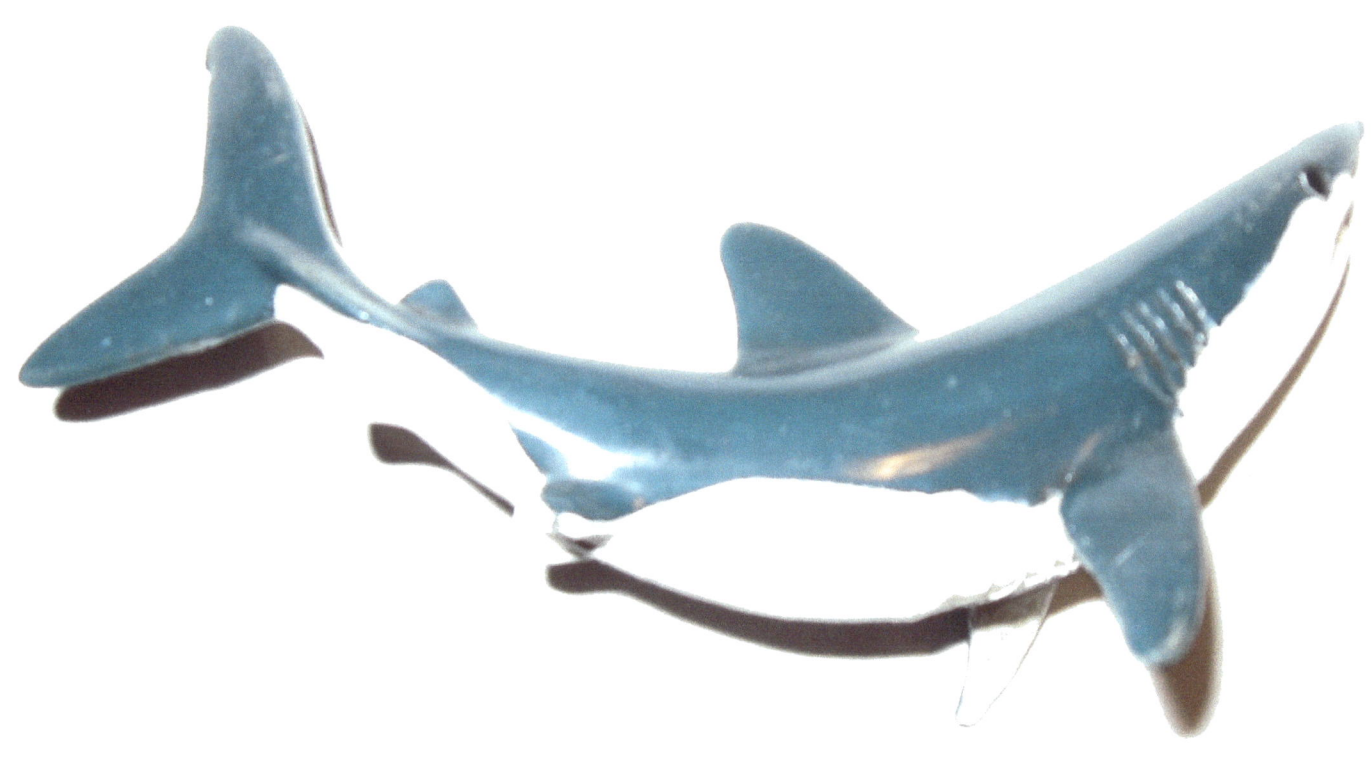

Toy sharks are a favorite of children.  But, they might not consider drawing or painting one!

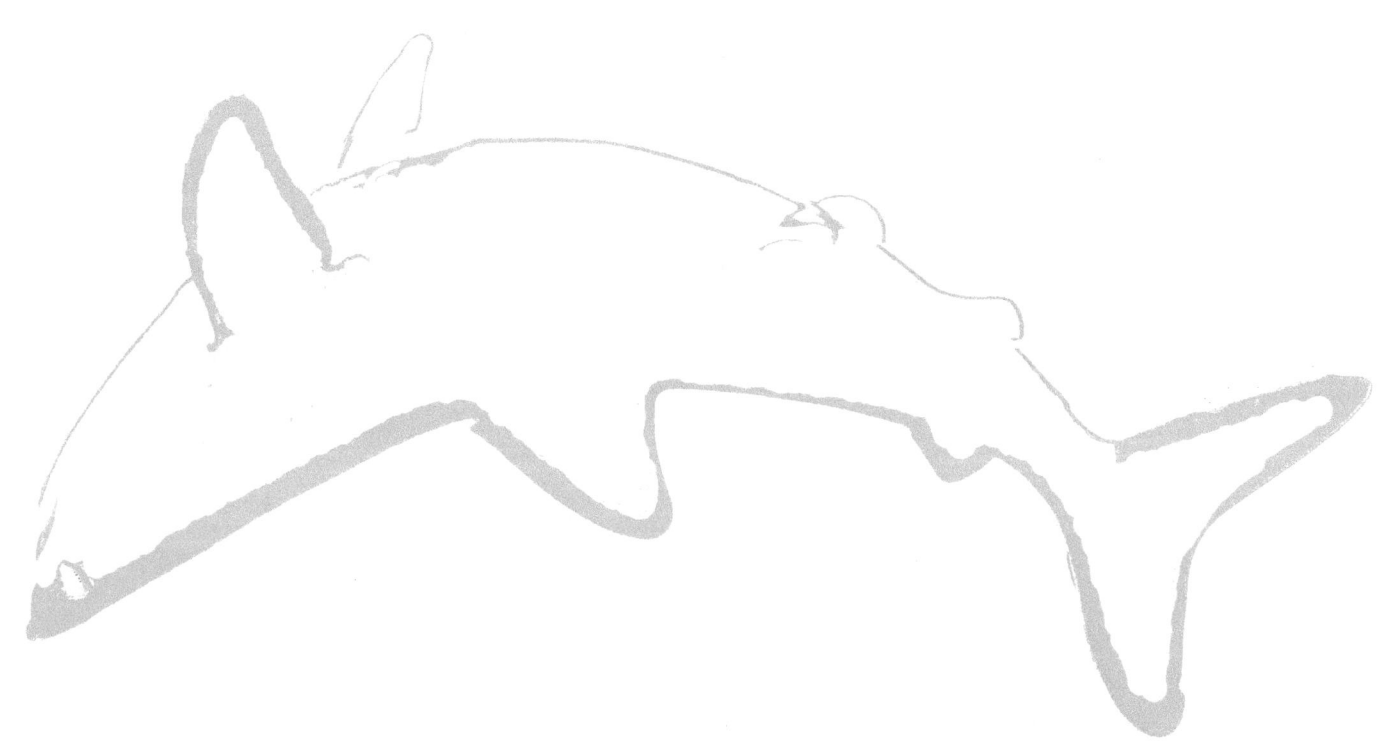

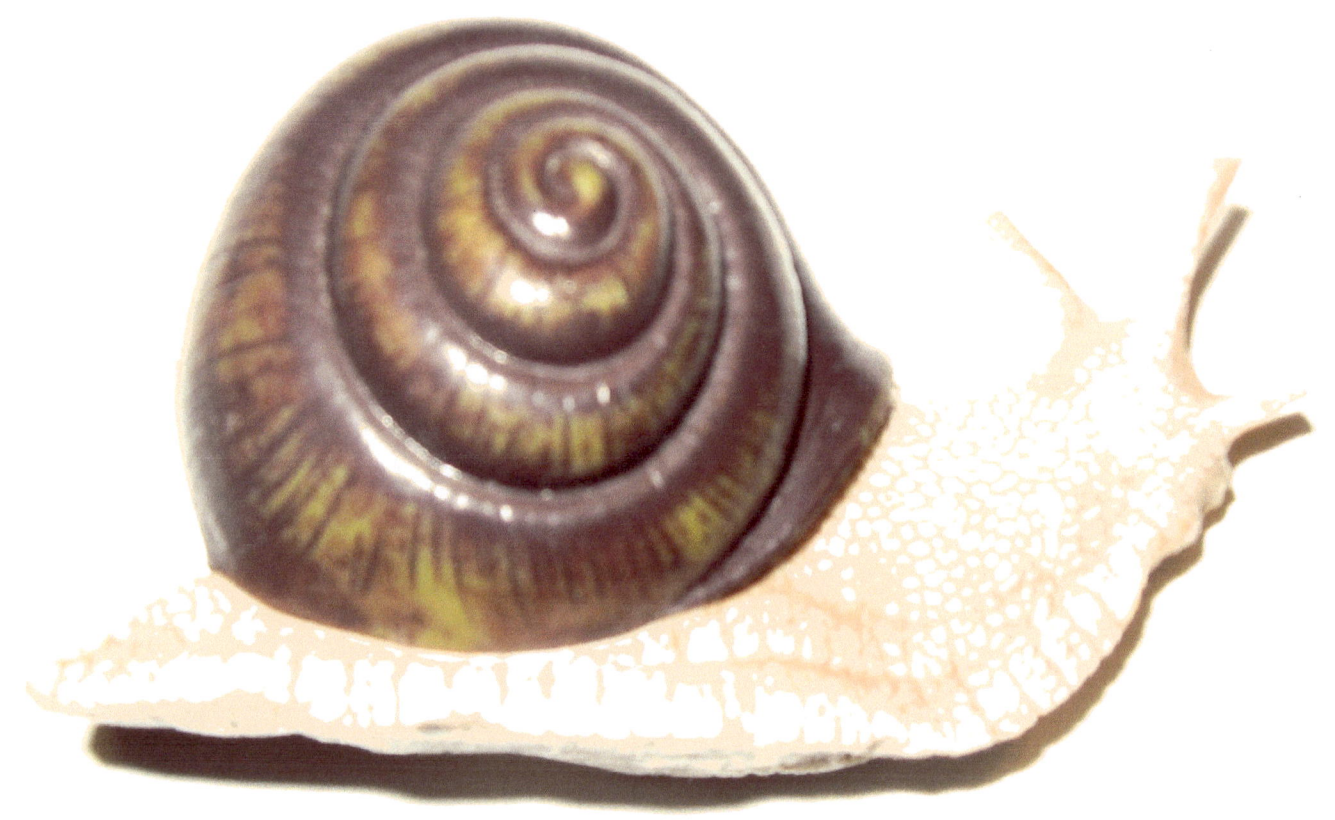

Are you up to the challenge of the snail shell's swirling spirals?

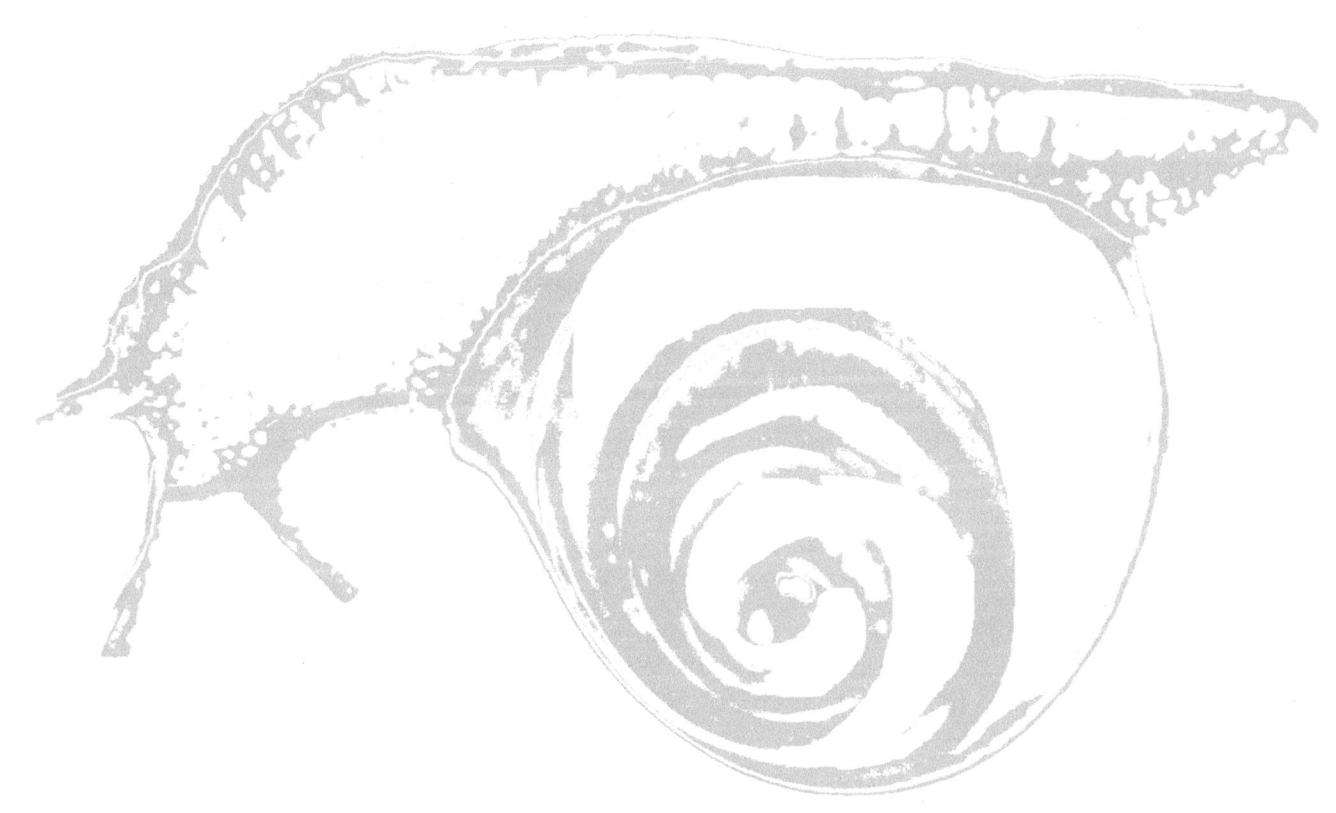

## A Few General Tips and Suggestions

Choose a medium not only for its finish, but also for ease of use; one that is comfortable for you.

Colored pencils are available in a wide variety of options, from simple and inexpensive school art pencils to costly, high quality pencils that can give the rich look of paint to your artwork. Watercolor pencils, with the tips dipped in water, release their depth of color in flowing, almost liquid application.

Paints can run the gamut from simple, bright tempera to hardy, moundable acrylic; from delicate watercolor to luxurious oils. Keep in mind that tempera, watercolors and even acrylics while still wet can be cleaned up with water, while oils require solvents or other mixtures created for that purpose.

Pastels, pen and ink, or charcoal add their own unique texture and appeal.

Experiment with various papers – size, weight and texture; canvas in linen or cotton, panels stretched and mounted, or multi-page canvas pads; even wood.

Mix colors to achieve life-like hues and tones. A few drops of glazing liquid helps to keep fast-drying acrylic paints moist, as well as add a hint of sheen to your colors.

Stark black or white can appear harsh and glaring. Add raw umber or burnt umber to black to help tone down black's natural harshness. In the same vein, instead of stark white for highlights, use slightly off-white colors or add a minuscule amount of raw umber to white to tone down the brightness.

In real life shadows are rarely a uniform black. For painting shadows, pull from deeper or more vibrant colors in nearby objects just the merest hint of that color.

Draw or paint in good light, in a pleasant, comfortable setting.

Foster in children a love of art by allowing them to freely express their unique perspective. Stick figures and "sky that covers only the top portion of a drawing" have their own special charm. And IF you encourage practice and bolster growing confidence these childlike efforts will gradually give way to more refined discernment, which will in turn translate into life-long works of high quality art.

***Above all remember that you want your artistic experience to reflect your inner vision, but to be enjoyable, not an onerous task!***

www.ingramcontent.com/pod-product-compliance
Lightning Source LLC
Chambersburg PA
CBHW050748180526
45159CB00003B/1383